Unreconciled?
Exploring mission in an imperfect world

Unreconciled?

Exploring mission in an imperfect world

Anne Richards

with the The Mission Theology Advisory Group

churches
together

IN BRITAIN AND IRELAND©

Churches Together in Britain and Ireland
39 Eccleston Square, London SW1V 1BX
www.ctbi.org.uk

ISBN 978-0-85169-369-9

Published 2011 by CTBI

Copyright © CTBI 2011

A catalogue record of this book is available from the British Library

Every effort has been made to verify the accuracy of previously published text, quotations and other material used in this book, and to obtain permissions where appropriate. The publishers will be pleased to rectify any errors or omissions in future editions of this book.

Further copies are available from:
Norwich Books and Music
13a Hellesdon Park Road
Norwich
Norfolk
NR6 5DR
www.norwichbooksandmusic.co.uk
01603 785925 T direct order line
01603 785915 F

Typeset in Adobe Minion with Hevetica Neue display
Design and production by Makar Publishing Production, Edinburgh

Printed and bound in Great Britain by Polestar Wheatons, Devon

Contents

Foreword

Bishop Leslie Hunter began his book *The Seed and the Fruit*[1] with a story:
'As the threats of war and the cries of dispossessed were sounding in his
ears, Western Man fell into an uneasy sleep. In his sleep he dreamed that
he had entered the spacious store in which the gifts of God to man are kept,
and addressed the angel behind the counter saying: "I have run out of the
fruits of the Spirit. Can you restock me?" When the angel seemed about to
say no, he burst out, "In place of war, afflictions, injustice, lying and lust, I
need love, joy, peace, integrity, discipline. Without these I shall be lost". And
the angel behind the counter replied, "We do not stock fruits, only seeds"'.

Globalization has radically altered the way people define themselves,
both individually and collectively. The development of competing narratives has brought a level of complexity unknown in previous times. The
World Wide Web has offered access to a global audience whose immediacy
sometimes allows individual and often extreme voices to drown out those
who work for quiet reconciliation. Reza Aslan comments that, 'In a world
where religion and politics are increasingly sharing the same vocabulary
and functioning in the same sphere, one can argue that religious grievances
are no less volatile than political grievances and religious violence no less
rational than political violence.'[2] We are encouraged to see others as oppo-
sites, especially those with a different ethnic identity or faith.

As we work through difficult times, the temptation is to reach for easy
answers and glib solutions. As many people compete for work and a decent
livelihood for their family it is all too easy to blame 'the other'. Yet we live
in a world of differences – of ideology, belief systems, ethnicity, social and
cultural values, whatever it might be. These differences are completely
natural. They're not something that we're going to be able to banish or get
rid of; diversity enriches our lives. What is important is how we deal with
these differences.

The need for reconciliation with our planet, as well as our neighbour,
becomes ever more pressing. The vast number of people moving around the
planet in search of food security and some small livelihood is daunting. The
Palestinian rights advocate Edward Said argues: 'our age, with its modern
warfare, imperialism and quasi-theological ambitions of totalitarian rulers...

---

1 Leslie Hunter (1953), *The Seed and the Fruit* (London: SCM), quoted in Peter Townley,
  'Sowing the Seeds of Mission on Stony Urban Soil', The Times Online December 2nd 2006
  at www.timesonline.co.uk/tol/comment/faith/article657114.ece.
2 Reza Aslan (2009), *How to Win a Cosmic War: God, Globalization and the End of the War on
  Terror*, (London: Random House) p. 16.

is indeed the age of the refugee, the displaced person, mass immigration' and he continues to point towards 'The unhealable rift forced between a human being and a native place, between the self and its true home'.[1]

Into this, Anne Richards reminds us that we are the people of the 'not yet' as Hebrews 11:1 tells us: 'Faith is the assurance of things hoped for, the conviction of things not yet seen.' All of us belong to the Unreconciled. That is why this book and set of resources is such an important milestone in the work that the churches need to do together. Only when we are confronting our own brokenness and our need for reconciliation can we in honesty and openness turn to our neighbour and build a good society with depth and compassion. The chapter headings within this book reveal to us the need to move from our own faith, identity and solid sense of self into relationships that build a good local, national and international community.

In this time when we are being confronted by radical spending cuts and an invitation to build strong local community this book is surely an important resource that can be used by local churches and church leaders to encourage a much greater sense of human flourishing. It is a reminder that we begin with ourselves and reach out to others. It is an invitation to engage with our neighbour and see within them the oneness that Christ prayed for. But that work will not be given to us, with easy solutions and ready-made narratives and outcomes. We must first recognize that we are Unreconciled and that we have to work with seeds not fruits.

Bob Fyffe
General Secretary
Churches Together in Britain and Ireland
November 2010

---

1 Edward Said (1990), 'Reflections on Exile' in Russell Ferguson, William Olander, Trinh T. Minh-Ha and Cornel West *Out There: Marginalisation and Contemporary Cultures*, (Cambridge, Mass: MIT Press) p. 357.

Preface

Turn on the television news and the broken and fragmented world comes to us in brilliant sound and vision. We see images of terrible wars, famine, disease and disaster. Some of these events are natural evils, some of them the result of human beings acting out of greed, wickedness, rage, revenge. Open a popular magazine and here are more personal events – celebrity marriages dissolving, sports personalities brawling, with attendant mud-slinging, misery and personal pain. Headline writers have plenty of emotive words to drag our eyes to the story: Agony, Anguish, Shame, Misery, Horror. There is a great deal of damage all around to fill up our thoughts and tug at our heart strings. There is plenty of information to talk, worry and gossip about.

What we may not consider though is the undercurrent of brokenness that simmers quietly away underneath what seems to be peace and quiet. Here, there are neighbours who have lived side by side for years, maybe generations, but whose history divides them forever and in ways that are never talked about until something makes it erupt into enmity. Here, are people living and working together for the greater good who, deep in their hearts, honestly believe their co-workers are inferior, or should not enjoy the rights they do, but who never voice their opinions or share their ideas, until one day one drink too many, or an unguarded email, brings it into the light. Here, is the child who, by chance, looks a bit different from all her peers and who is avoided by other children at school. Here, are the people dealt with by democratic and peaceful societies who are shut away or forgotten by ordinary people who enjoy freedoms unknown by these lost others.

Every single one of us lives in this imperfect world, and we know from our own experience that the world is not as it ought to be, or could be. For Christians this disparity between how things are and how they could be, fuels the desire to find out what God's intention is for the creation, to discover how we can do God's will and commit ourselves to working for that better world. This requires both sharing our faith in Jesus Christ in order to tell others about God's desire for human beings, and working for change, transformation and care for our world. This is mission.

There is a great deal written about mission and about transforming work, but we tend to take less notice of the place all of us start from and what effect living in an imperfect world has on who *we* are. Each of us exists in a world that is not yet reconciled to God's will. Even though as Christians, we 'wait for adoption' as Paul puts it (Romans 8.23, see in context 18–35), and believe in the certainty of God's promises, yet our situation, as a community of all human beings, is to belong to an unreconciled world that is not yet characterised by equality, peace and justice. The prayer that Jesus taught us and which the Church uses in every act of worship emphasises this point: 'Thy kingdom come'. We are the people of the 'not yet' as Hebrews 11:1 tells us: 'Faith is the assurance of things hoped for...the conviction of things not yet seen.' All of us belong to the Unreconciled.

In this book, we purposely use the word Unreconciled, with a capital letter, as a jar and a reminder of our common condition. In the chapters which follow we look at particular groups of Unreconciled people, but it would be easy to slip into an 'us' and 'them' perspective, where we lament the state people are in and seek to help them, without realising that they mirror for us what is also true for ourselves. The word Unreconciled, every time it appears, calls us to account and recalls us to our duty as Christians to see our common humanity in our neighbours around us, to hear their stories and enable them to enter with us into whatever kinds of reconciling action may be appropriate. Our title, with its question mark, reminds us never to take for granted that we have done enough to resolve an issue, that everything in the garden is now rosy. Reconciliation is not something that happens once and can then be considered finished. It takes work, effort, energy and a real commitment to ongoing transformation.

This means that this is not straightforwardly a book 'about' reconciliation. There are in fact many insightful books about reconciliation and about reconciliation in relation to Christian mission,[1] but one of the problems in thinking and writing about reconciliation is that it becomes a treatment of the symptoms of a broken world without spending time deep in the wounds looking at and wondering about the disease itself. Because we do not habitually think of ourselves as the Unreconciled, we ignore the fact that we too are quite capable of strengthening the Unreconciled state, pushing people further away, trapping them in places where it seems impossible that reconciling action can liberate them. So, for example, the exclusion of the homeless or mentally ill, masks a society which is deeply insecure about its identity and measures 'success' by 'ownership' of property and assets. Whilst condemning obesity and addiction, we fail to acknowledge the general drive of consumption or *pleonexia* (see Luke 12.13–21) – the desire within all of us to have or acquire more. The (rightful) condemnation of those who carry out sexual abuse of any kind, masks a society which is by many standards, over sexualised. Unless we can approach such marginalised people who are our brothers and sisters, understand what has happened to them and take action to release them, we cannot understand our own Unreconciled condition or seek reconciliation for ourselves.

For example in Matthew 25.31–46, Jesus tells the story of those people

---

1 We provide suggestions for further reading at the end of this book.

coming for judgement who are deemed to have served him: 'I was hungry and you gave me food, I was thirsty and you gave me something to drink, I was a stranger and you welcomed me, I was naked and you gave me clothing, I was sick and you took care of me, I was in prison and you visited me'. Everyone is perplexed by these words and asks when it was that Jesus could have been in such situations, but Jesus reveals that such a powerful relationship and reconciliation with God is deeply ingrained into every occasion when people respond to others found in such conditions: 'Truly I tell you, just as you did it to one of the least of these who are members of my family, you did it to me.' The reconciliation that occurs (or not) in this story is directly related to personal empathy and reaction to other groups of Unreconciled people. Actions such as these undo the ills which work against God's purposes by provoking empathy with hunger, thirst, being ill, or feeling like a stranger. The self-knowledge which comes with giving and caring actions fits people for life with God.

Dave[1]

This man comes to the door and asks for money. He was a beggar like. I didn't like the look of him to be honest and I said I didn't have any money, which was true. But then I looked at him some more and I could see he was starving. Then suddenly I remembered during the war when our street was bombed and we were trying to put things back together. There wasn't any food that day and I was so hungry. I kept whining and whining at my mother. Then all our neighbours got together and made a meal for everyone out of all we had left and what came in from outside. I remembered I was so glad to get that food. So then I made the man some jam sandwiches and he sat in the garden and ate them. And he told me he had been in a war and that was why he was here. We both remembered the bombs and the destruction.

In each chapter in this book the heart of the issue is stories of those people who are separated, far off, lost or cast away, for whatever reasons. Their stories reach out to us, demanding that we respond to them without the precondition of an easy cure, but first with empathy and a search for understanding as Dave does in the story above. When we ask the question 'what is it like to be one of *these* Unreconciled?' we have to find out about the particular circumstances of people around us and so gain insight into our own unreconciled lives. In investigating groups of Unreconciled in our communities we learn what is it like to stand among them and alongside them and to know what kinship we have with them. If we strip away all the presuppositions and assumptions we have about 'other people', with the problems and difficulties we first think can never be ours, we find that

---

1 A number of people have entrusted us with their stories and allowed us to use them. To protect their privacy, we have changed their names.

there are extraordinary stories which tell us profound things about being human and which throw our easy ideas about Christian mission into question. The different groups of Unreconciled prompt us to ask what shapes reconciliation can take that can lift them and us out of the Unreconciled state and give back dignity and humanity. We then have to dig hard into our ideas about reconciling action and to ask what kind of reconciliation can (if at all) make a difference or bring about transformation. In this book, with its explorations at global, national, local and deeply personal level, we can try to find out.

We start by offering a view of God's world which has disorder and decay built into its processes and reflect on what reconciliation means in such a context. Two chapters concern explicitly theological matters, a God's eye view, as it were, of the problems of a world which is inhabited and stewarded by the deeply Unreconciled. These reflections are intended to provide a framework from which to probe more deeply into various particular worlds of Unreconciled people and our own part in putting and keeping them there.

The process of compiling the material for this book has been helped by seeking out people whose lives have been touched and changed by contact with various groups of Unreconciled people, but more than this, those people have lived in solidarity with such groups, become them, made their stories their own. In the course of producing this book, we in the Mission Theology Advisory Group have heard a great deal of passionate testimony and have also been made aware that any attempt to talk about these issues is only scratching the surface of a very complex and difficult set of problems. The task has been to reflect theologically on this testimony and try to make sense of it. While many of MTAG's partners in this process have been professionals and experts, members of the group have also spent time in the community talking to ordinary people, like Dave above, about what reconciliation means to them in their daily lives. Those voices are scattered throughout the text, unvarnished stories of simple reflection on what the word 'reconciliation' might mean. The responses have been touching, surprising, worrying, encouraging, but each reminds us that you don't have to be a theologian, a member of the clergy, or even a Christian, to discern what God is doing in daily life.

The Mission Theology Advisory Group

MTAG is an ecumenical partnership which brings together people nominated by the Mission and Public Affairs Division of the Archbishops' Council of the Church of England and people nominated by Churches Together in Britain and Ireland. Our job is to advise and resource the churches on issues of Christian mission in today's world.

For this project, members of MTAG were as follows:
The Rt Revd Dr David Atkinson (co-chair of MTAG)
The Revd Professor John Drane (co-chair of MTAG)
Dr Nicholas Adams
Mr Andrew Brookes
The Rt Revd Dr Brian Castle
The Revd Canon Joanna Penberthy
Canon Janice Price
The Revd Dr Israel Selvanayagam
The Revd Dr David Spriggs
The Revd Dr Andrew Wood

Members and staff of the current MTAG group have also commented and shaped the material including:
The Revd Ben Edson
The Revd Bob Fyffe
Dr Kirsteen Kim
The Revd Dr Victoria Johnson
Ms Alison Webster

We were helped by a number of consultants who graciously gave us the benefit of their time and expertise in developing different chapters and we offer our grateful thanks to:
The Revd Professor Sebastian Kim (*Separation and Unity*)
The Very Revd Dr Andrew McLellan CBE (*Punishment and Liberation*)
Fr Jim McManus (*Condemnation and Forgiveness*)
The Revd Professor Piet Meiring (*Lies and Truth*)
The Revd David Porter (*Separation and Unity*)
The Revd Philip Roderick (*Speaking and Listening*)

We also want to thank the Revd Canon Andrew White who corresponded with us while he was in Baghdad.

We are grateful to David McLeod of Makar Publishing for the design and layout of this book, and also thank Mary Gandy of CTBI for handling the permissions.

The material in this book was written and prepared by Dr Anne Richards, the secretary to the group, to whom any enquiries should be made.

Contact:
Dr Anne Richards
Mission and Public Affairs
Archbishops' Council
Church House
Great Smith Street
London
SW1P 3AZ
0207 8981444
anne.richards@churchofengland.org

How to use this book

+ This book can be used for private study and reflection. Some chapters may be more relevant than others to your own situation and you may wish to concentrate on these. Otherwise you can work through the chapters for a general reflection and study of the Unreconciled in our world. You may like to use the study materials at the end of the book for ideas, activities, reflections and prayer.

+ This book also contains a complete set of study materials for use with groups. There are opportunities to explore using discussion questions, Bible studies, activities which engage local communities, as well as prayers and reflections. These materials can be found at the end of the book, together with notes for group leaders, starting on page 140.

+ A Lent Course based on this book and containing a complete set of resources for study and reflection throughout the Lenten period is available at www.ctbi.org.uk and at the MTAG website www.spiritualjourneys.org.uk.

Introduction

The world is running down

'When clouds are full
They empty rain upon the earth;
whether a tree falls to the south or to the north
In the place where the tree falls,
there it will lie'
Ecclesiastes 11.3

Living with mess

Scientists tell us that it is a given feature of our world, and indeed of the universe in which we live, that disorder always increases over time. So systems run down and never start up again by themselves. Whatever is ordered becomes disordered and chaotic. Drop your soup on the floor and it will become disordered – not to say messy! But you would wait forever for the broken china to jump back together again and the spilled liquid to pour itself back into the dish, beautifully ordered and ready for you to eat. Once you have dropped your soup, there is nothing you can do but clear it up. For things to remain as they are energy has to be continuously added to stop disorder taking over.

We don't need scientists to tell us what this feels like in daily life. If we don't organise our lives, clean, maintain and repair, things fall into decay. If we don't have our cars serviced they will eventually fail to work, our houses need to be looked after, cracks plastered, roof tiles mended. If you lose a shirt button, it will not put itself back on unless you mend it. Our lives are shot through with the attention needed to put energy into keeping order and preventing the rise of disorder around us.

So we are used to the idea that at the physical level we have to spend our energy keeping things from falling into chaos. We never encounter the world as a perfect existence where we can just *be*; we have to spend our lives *doing* things. The world we know is not the dreamy paradise of the Garden of Eden, where everything just is, the world we know is on the other side of the gate where Adam and Eve are toiling away making clothes and growing food to stop themselves starving and freezing to death. Yet nature, although subject to time and disorder (St Paul talks about 'bondage to decay' in Romans 8.21), is not in itself an unreconciled environment. Nitrogen, carbon, water and rocks recycle over time. Animal and plant populations wax and wane. Evolution forges subtle dependencies between creatures who make a living, multiply and fill the earth with marvellous diversity. It is only as human beings start to have a profound impact on nature that we notice the unbalancing and destruction of the environment – and one which is fast getting away from our attempts to restore the balance. The world of the fallen Adam and Eve is the world of the Unreconciled, but today even the environment in which we know ourselves Unreconciled is contaminated by our presence. St Paul perhaps speaks prophetically, as well as immediately, when he continues in Romans 8.22 about the creation 'groaning in labour pains' and waiting for redemption.

Christians therefore talk about living in a fallen world, a world which is not as God desires it. But fallenness does not just refer to the way order constantly decays to disorder, or even to the damage we have done to the environment, though that is grave sin. The fallen world contains other layers of damage and destruction. The story of the Garden of Eden gives us further clues about this. Adam and Eve don't just end up in a world which is running down, but take with them the knowledge of evil and suffering, a knowledge which is born of their new status as the Unreconciled, parted by their actions from just being in the continuous blessed presence of God. This means that if being human requires us continually to work to combat disorder, to restore balance, to *reconcile*, then that work must also include paying attention to the way we resist and try to overcome those things which cause evil and suffering.[1]

So the largest community of the Unreconciled is simply the community of all human beings. We are Eves and Adams, living, as we must, on the other side of paradise. In such a world, all kinds of things happen which bring grief and pain, from the enormity of a tsunami disaster or the massive earthquake in Haiti, to a local road accident; from appalling famine and disease to a struggle with illness in the family. Yet we are not helpless in these situations. The story of Adam and Eve tells us that when human beings *recognise* their Unreconciled state they discover that God has given them gifts of intelligence, creativity, positive thinking, the ability to recognise beauty and the vision to imagine and cherish a better world.[2]

'Lay your sleeping head my love
Human on my faithless arm;
Time and fevers burn away
Individual beauty from
Thoughtful children and the grave proves
The child ephemeral:

---

1 Three of the 'marks' of mission (see page 5) refer to this work: to respond to human need by love and service; to seek to transform unjust structures of society; to respect the integrity of creation and to sustain and renew the earth. A new mark of mission has also explicitly been formulated in 2010 to address issues of peace, conflict resolution and reconciliation.

2 So in C. S. Lewis' *The Lion, the Witch and the Wardrobe*, for example, we find Edmund driven by his own 'messy' desires to betray his family and friends, yet journeying to reconciliation as everyone moves beyond what divides to what finally binds them together.

But in my arms till break of day
Let the living creature lie,
Mortal, guilty, but to me,
The entirely beautiful'
W. H. Auden, *Lullaby*[1]

We have to live with mess and change, we can fall short, be 'faithless' and 'guilty' and we shall certainly all die in the end anyway – but the human capacity to love can transform anything and everything. As Christians we also know that human love is a reflection of divine love continually poured into the creation. So when Adam and Eve leave their perfect world, God goes with them and a new relationship begins in which we can use our gifts freely to help God make things new. We can see this because when dreadful things happen, we also hear how people respond to put their energy into 'trying to help' or 'doing good'. The terrible tragedy of the Haiti earthquake in January 2010 immediately brought international offers of help and response from charities and aid agencies, including (for example) an immediate initial £50,000 donation from the Salvation Army. Whether it is caring for a sick person at home, or being part of an international charity trying to combat the AIDS pandemic, we understand instinctively that the will to do good, to rebuild, to comfort and to heal can overcome the sense that we are helpless in the face of overwhelming destructive forces.

The tremendous response that people are capable of in time of suffering, war or disaster, not to mention in the smaller tragedies that affect people in their own homes, show that it's really not the human way to say 'what's the point?' and turn our backs on it. In the book of Job, we see a human being endlessly tested in this way. Ruin and disorder wreck Job's life, but he refuses to give up and die: 'I will hold fast my righteousness, and will not let it go; my heart does not reproach me for any of my days' (Job 27.6). This is because human beings are capable of looking further than immediate experience, no matter how desperate, and carry the hope of a better future. Despite his afflictions and miseries, Job refuses to cast himself into despair. Towards the end of the book, God reveals to him a picture of the magnificence and wonder of the world we are incapable of recreating by ourselves and within which human beings have a particular and beloved place. Only by entering into this mystery can Job emerge on the other side of his suffering and rebuild his life.

Like Job, we are also aware that damage and disorder occur in the way we live our lives despite the best laid plans of mice and men. The clear vision we would like to live by gets muddied. Dreams never materialise, lies get told, relationships break down, a child dies, the clarity of faith wavers, people are betrayed, mistreated, or ignored. For anyone involved

---

1 Copyright © 1976, 1991. The Estate of W.H. Auden.

in ministry, these things are part of the ministerial task: pastoral care, counselling, comforting, helping and praying in the face of the dream of a happy, peaceful life that one day got shattered. But this is also part of the general Christian task, to build, create, redeem, make new. Once we know ourselves as Unreconciled, we can also be certain that we are endowed with the capability to make a difference, change the world and seek redemption. How does this happen, and what effect does it have on the world around us? Further, what about those people who are trapped in a state where none of those gifts can be used?

More than cleaners
In the film *Bruce Almighty*, God (played by Morgan Freeman) is a humble and overlooked cleaner, quietly and eternally sweeping up human mess, while Bruce goes out squandering his power on his own petty and selfish

wants. When most people think about the word 'reconciliation', they often tend to think of it as what is required to address damage; like Morgan Freeman's God, they imagine rolling up their sleeves to clear up endless heartbreaking mess. The word reconciliation comes from the Latin *reconciliare*, from *conciliare* which means to 'bring together'. In typical use it means to restore friendly relations between, to make or show to be compatible, or to make someone accept a disagreeable thing. So when people use the word reconciliation they mean to put differences away and to make up; it means to heal a breach, to get two people talking again, to mend a broken part in a relationship. In this sense, we always assume the damage first, the breakdown that needs to be repaired. We look at our dropped soup and wonder how we are going to clear up the mess.

However, the theological concept of reconciliation has *more* to it than this and because it is more than mere repair, it is both a prophetic act and a profoundly missionary event. This aspect of reconciliation is often overlooked by Christians, not least those involved in mission. We start thinking that mission is only about sorting out problems rather than creating something new. The five marks of mission[1] imply that creative forces need to be at work: we are called to *transform* unjust structures and *renew* the earth. We therefore want to argue that Christian reconciliation is not about repair (although it might involve repair) but a *bringing to birth of something new* out of the Unreconciled condition. When reconciliation touches the lives of the Unreconciled, something unexpected can occur that involves all of us in a transformation, irrespective of whether the reconciling process results in a good outcome or not.

What have we got that will enable us to deal with the effects of what Christians refer to as personal and structural sin? Some philosophers would say that it is simply the will to Good – that most reasonable human beings want to turn aside from anarchy and chaos and have peaceful, co-operative and just lives. Christians can be even clearer. We have a capacity to use our gifts and our energy to address the needs of the Unreconciled around us who cannot for whatever reason find the energy for themselves. We can argue theologically that the energy that is released in mission and released through the worship of almighty God, comes from Jesus and is operative in the world by means of the Holy Spirit. Thus Christians are gifted in this way to make a particular difference through God's gracious gift to us. If we *don't* do this, we can be as bad as Job's comforters, who spend their time debating what sin he has committed to suffer in this way, without doing anything to help except make him feel worse.

---

1 These are: to proclaim the Good News of the kingdom; to teach, nurture and baptise new believers; to respond to human need by loving service; to seek to transform unjust structures of society; to respect the integrity of creation and to sustain and renew the earth. Interestingly, the latest, sixth 'mark' introduced in 2010 expressly includes reconciliation: 'To work for peace-making, conflict resolution and reconciliation'.

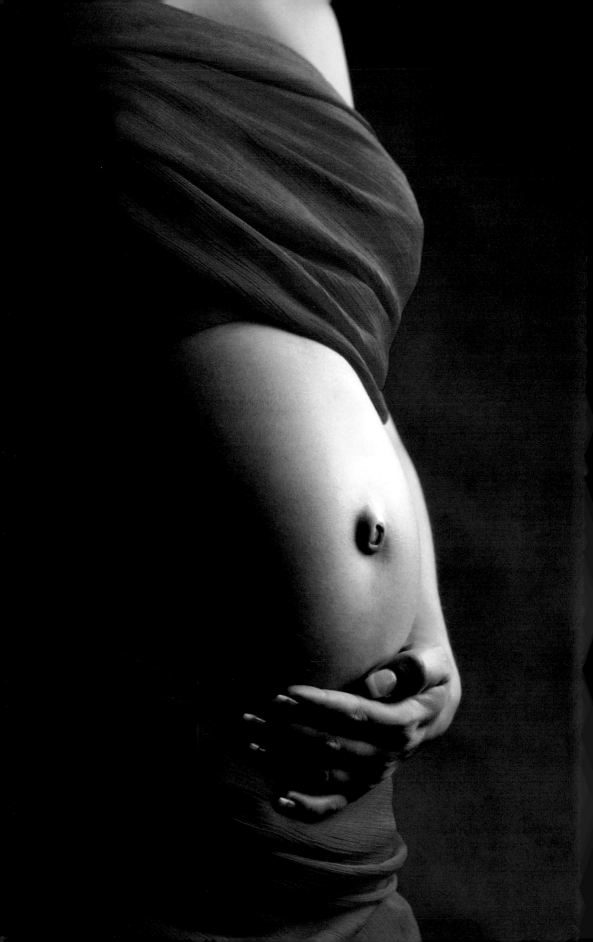

Reconciliation as pregnancy and birth

The Taiwanese theologian C. S. Song describes the reconciliation God has made possible in this world using the image of a womb. For him, the suffering of Asian people through conflict requires an image of hope and this is found in biblical images of God's planting a seed of life in the barren womb. The barren womb is, in human terms, past all hope, but for God all things are possible. For Song, then, the miracle of Sarah, Abraham's wife, conceiving a child in old age (Genesis 17.15–21; Hebrews 11.11), is symbolic of the seed of renewed hope and possibility for Unreconciled Asian people.[1]

If we take this concept further and develop it, we can see that reconciliation in the mission of the Church requires first an understanding that God desires to bring order into our disordered world and invites our help to do it. The barren woman, who longs for a child, is a type of the Unreconciled. She is physically subject to the disorder of time and age as well as to the breakdown of positive vision and hope. Despite her potential and her desire, nothing happens to allow her to realise it. God provides the seed of life, by the action of the Holy Spirit, even deep within what appears to be beyond all possibility or all hope. Our task is to accede to this life-giving and reconciling action, to nurture that seed and to bring it to birth. Such birthing will not be without difficulty or hard work, but the new thing which is brought into the world will be evidence of God's desire to renew, re-make and restore what we thought had been lost or was irrecoverable. It is unsurprising then, that the joy of barren women who conceive children in the Hebrew Scriptures is heard again in the story of the Incarnation of Christ, God's son. This is the ultimate form of creative reconciling work, where the seed that is planted in the womb of humanity is God's own self. To commit ourselves to reconciliation in mission then, is to agree to become pregnant with God's creative desire and to devote ourselves to nurturing it among the Unreconciled and bringing it to birth.

Expecting his angel

Reconciliation contains within it the essence of hope and also surprise and possibility, of new and quite unexpected things, like the vision offered to Job, or the promise offered to Mary. This reminds us that we should give up many of our presuppositions and assumptions about mission and not imagine limits or restrictions on reconciliation. Rather we should expect the reconciliatory force of mission to bring new things, surprising things, visionary and prophetic things, into the world. As Christians we should expect God to offer us the chance to create something new at all levels of our human lives. But how many of us wait in expectation of God's angel and how many of us miss that angel even when he is standing in the middle of

---

1 See, for example, C. S. Song (1979), *Third Eye Theology: Theology in Formation in Asian Settings* (Maryknoll, NY: Orbis Books); (1986) *Theology from the Womb of Asia* (Maryknoll, NY: Orbis Books).

our pathway? Part of the problem, the reason why we miss God's angel, is that we have not dealt with our own Unreconciled situation or with the issue of the Unreconciled among us, whom society expects us to curse, but God requires us to bless (see Numbers 22).

In this book, the task is to raise awareness of the status of the Unreconciled, of our own unreconciled nature and the presence of the Unreconciled among us, many of whom are paralysed by history, by evil acts, by being trapped by circumstance or human actions upon them. This book argues that offering solidarity with the Unreconciled who cannot help themselves is the first act in relating Christian mission to justice. This book then looks at what sort of reconciling acts are possible and defines reconciliation as acts, or processes, which work against moral and spiritual disorder and the effects of human sin. The effects of such reconciling work are hope and possibility. The products of such reconciling work are new creations, beyond mere repair. This book also argues that mission is powered by reconciliation and that Christian mission is dependent on energy being invested in such reconciling work. It looks at issues of the Unreconciled in expectation of God's angel, calling us to incarnate the reconciling seed in those places and in those human hearts. The work of nurture and growth of this seed is revealed as mission.

This books further aims to show what the links are between the acts and processes of reconciliation and the missionary task of the Church in relation to the myriad Unreconciled among us. In each chapter, a group of Unreconciled people who have been oppressed or damaged provides the focus for an exploration of what kinds of reconciliation seek to address that damage and create something new. Reconciliation is considered in terms of what it adds to the mission of the Church and to the way in which the Church offers its purpose and vision of the Kingdom to the people of the world and indeed to the whole creation. For each chapter birth metaphors are used to think about how to help these groups of Unreconciled people move from their state using the following questions:

Where is the seed of life?

How will we carry it?

Where can it be born?

How can we nurture it?

What will we hope to see?

Humanity and God

Reconciliation at the heart of God's being

If the Unreconciled are everywhere among us, and if we too are the Unreconciled, then how is it possible to bring to birth the seed of creative reconciliation that God plants in us? What is it about the nature of God that provides a model for Christian reconciliation? How does this reconciling nature relate to concepts of God's mission, the *missio dei*? The answer is that we learn about the reconciling work of God in a number of ways.

First, Scripture gives us a picture of God perpetually interested and involved in the heart of creation. The creation as we know it today is beautiful and wonderful, but also damaged and broken by human beings as rainforests are ravaged or oil from the Deepwater Horizon offshore rig spills into the sea; it is the home of the Unreconciled. God's desire then, is for the world to be restored so that it can display its unbroken diversity and beauty and this can only happen through reconciling work. We are told through Scripture that God's intention towards the creation is to reconcile the creation to his own self. What does this mean?

A picture of a primordial perfect creation is implicit in the creation stories in Genesis. God creates and celebrates the essential goodness and rightness of what has been created. The material universe is perfect and beautiful reflecting entirely God's desire and intention. The Garden of Eden and its inhabitants live in a landscape which is infused by God and entirely referential of God. For as long as the inhabitants align their freedom and will with that of God's desire for them that state of perfection where human and divine will exactly mirror each other remains intact. The difficulty of course, is that being human means being reflective, curious, wilful, experimental. Faced not just with choice but with temptation, humans are not able to maintain a state of blissful perfection for very long, but as Genesis shows, the very traits which get them expelled from the Garden are the ones which enable them to survive outside it.

As soon as human beings begin to introduce self-seeking will and actions into their world, the creation is left to be redesigned in some ways that pave the way back to God and some which exclude God's loving desire and depart from God's purposes. Humans can choose to employ their freedom and will to carve out new paths away from the shelter of divine love, just as the Prodigal sets out on his journey to ruin (Luke 15.11–32). Once this happens, we are in the country of the Unreconciled as strangers and pilgrims and bound by our new choices we become less free than God intends.

God's reconciling work therefore includes freeing us from the knots we get ourselves into and giving us back our true freedom. So theology argues that God, patient as the Father in Jesus' parable of the Prodigal Son, never ceases from attempting to restore the creation to its perfect state, liberating human beings to be free as they were meant to be. Jesus' picture is of a dynamic, loving Father who waits and hopes, always searching the horizon for the beloved, ready always to heal the breach and celebrate the loved one's homecoming. So we can say unequivocally that no matter what we do, God loves the world and God never gives up. In Scripture, Jesus tells us that we should pay attention to the sign of Jonah (Matthew 12.38–41).

The sign of Jonah

In the book of Jonah, in the Hebrew Scriptures, we hear the story of a man called by God, chosen and desired by God to be part of God's mission. He is chosen for a task of going to the Unreconciled, who in this case are the people of Ninevah, and proclaiming God's message among them. Jonah does not want to hear this call or respond to this invitation, and so runs away into turmoil and disaster, becoming himself one of the same group of Unreconciled, deliberately putting himself far away from God. His status as one of the Unreconciled immediately becomes visible in external events. Instead of peace and harmony there is storm and fear. Jonah is called a cursed person, a bringer of bad luck and destruction. But God pursues Jonah with saving love. Like the people of Ninevah, he will not be passed over or given up as a hopeless cause. Everyone knows the story of Jonah swallowed and restored to dry land by the whale, but that striking Sunday school story carries the implication that God will go to the very depths to find us and save us. As Jonah himself says:

> 'the waters closed in over me;
> the deep surrounded me;
> weeds were wrapped around my head
> at the roots of the mountains.
> I went down to the land
> whose bars closed upon me forever;
> yet you brought up my life from the Pit,
> O Lord my God.'
> Jonah 2.5–6

Jesus tells us, with prophetic intent lacing his words that God will send his servant into the further depths of hell to bring us home.[1]

If we listen to Jesus' words and pay attention to the sign of Jonah we notice two things. One is that the *missio dei* (the mission of God's love to the world) is by definition a dynamic reconciling work, to which all human beings are called to be partners in sharing. Secondly, Christians believe that

---

1 See our chapter on 'Hell and Heaven'.

that reconciling work reaches its epitome in the person and work of Jesus Christ. If we want to know more about God's work, intention and desire for people like us, it is to the gospel of Jesus Christ that we must go.

Jesus teaches us more about God's reconciling work by talking about God not as a monolithic divinity cut off and separate from creation, but constantly overcoming barriers and breakdowns in dynamic and active ways. God constantly makes it possible for us to be in relationship, through love, through fellowship, through communication. The establishment of such relationship is part of the reconciling work that is intended to involve us all in God's community. In the west, we still tend to have such monolithic views, not only of God, but of ourselves. We often see ourselves as individuals separated from others; we lived in an individualised society. Some non-western theologies, however, would argue that we can also see ourselves as community. From each one of us there are extensions of relationship in love and friendship, to parents, children, aunts, uncles, friends and neighbours. Those extensions are just as much 'us' as the sense of being an individual person. Family and community are also descriptions of 'us'. Furthermore, every conversation we have with another offers us into a new relationship of dialogue, so that we become bundles of dialogue, interchanges and networks that are also 'us'.

Jade

When I went to Uni I soon made loads of new friends and some of them were Muslims and Sikhs and Christians. The Christians were going off to services and all that and they kept asking me to go with them. I didn't go, but I did wonder what it would be like. I talked to the chaplain a bit too and I really liked him and thought he was an easy person to talk to about relationships and stuff. When I went home at the end of term I told my family that I had made Christian friends and talked to the chaplain and they were really worried and upset. They didn't want me to go back. I was really upset and crying and I wrote that I was really upset on Facebook. And all my friends wrote things on my wall, sending me hugs and support. Some of them phoned me and said I could go and stay with them, but some of the others said I should make it up with my family. And I decided that I would try and get my mum and dad to meet some of my friends, just all sit down and have a big meal together, just talking about the ordinary stuff, not religion.

This combination of face to face relationships and social networking is something that is challenging the individualistic view, as we use the computer for interaction through Facebook, Twitter, Bebo, MySpace, online forums and discussion communities and the like.

Jesus' disciples and followers form an extending community, and the Church also. God, as Father, Son and Holy Spirit, demonstrates just such love, fellowship and communication within the divine life (*perichoresis*) and this is poured out into the creation helping to create more community and more dialogue. Thus, in Acts, we not only have the day of Pentecost but many conversions, as the community grows and becomes ever more intricately linked through love and fellowship. This is God's reconciling work in action, but, as we know, and as was evident in the early church, human beings have many ways of wilfully undoing such work and messing it up again. The Pauline letters point to worries about the way human wilfulness, pride and discord undo community and set neighbour against neighbour, friend against friend. Against God's reconciling work, creating community, love and friendship, we constantly create different communities of the Unreconciled.

God's longing and human longing

Yet God never gives up. God longs for reconciliation with the creation so that that it can be restored to unity with, and inclusion in the divine life. The longing of God for reconciliation is made known to us through God's activity. Scripture, as well as the long history of religious testimony, records how God never ceases from reconciling work in the world. The Hebrew Scriptures tell us about God's relationship with the people of Israel; Jesus teaches us about the work of the Father who is out looking for us, waiting for us to come home; the Holy Spirit guides and inspires the people of God. God's longing for the whole of creation, spills over into the *pleroma* of Ephesians 3.19, the 'fullness' of God, a forgiving love that pours into the world for eternity.[1]

As creatures made in the image of the Triune God, Father, Son and Holy Spirit, the human psyche also contains within it the possibility of experiencing longing for what is not itself. People experience this longing in all sorts of ways. We may desire material things and to surround ourselves with accoutrements, but the majority of human beings also desire love, happiness, strong, binding relationships with others, and ultimately a sense of connection and belonging to some ultimate destiny.

> 'Courage, emotional imagination and humility enable us to open up to another in ways that enable both of us to become more of what we can be. The skills of intimacy are crucial to the creative building of human identity because they are the skills of human connection, and connection gives us access to the "we". The more we access the "we", the more fully human we become'.[2]

Some religions require adherents to divorce themselves from attachments and desires; Christianity asks us to distinguish between different attachments and so recognise that the desire for relationship mirrors the desire God has for us. Longing is therefore built into the mission of the

---

1 This idea is picked up in one of the Church of England's Eucharistic Prayers: 'Though we chose the path of rebellion, you would not abandon your own. Again and again you drew us into your covenant of grace.' Eucharistic Prayer F.

2 Alison Webster, (2009) *You are Mine, Reflections on Who We Are* (London: SPCK), p. 41.

Church – we long to see others be received into the Father's house, feasting and celebrating. We long for hurt and sorrow to be taken away. We long to see others accept Jesus' offer and lay down their burdens. The work of the Holy Spirit in us, reminding us of the ache of God for the creation, drives all true evangelism and is a deeply reconciling work. Similarly, we can recognise that many groups of the Unreconciled are precisely those whose longing for connection and relationship is thwarted and many such people live close to us every day.

> I can do nothing else than endure in the face of this deepest and most painful of mysteries. I believe in God the Father Almighty, maker of heaven and earth and resurrecter of Jesus Christ. I also believe that my son's life was cut off in its prime. I cannot fit these pieces together. I am at a loss. I have read the theodicies produced to justify the ways of God to man. I find them unconvincing. To the most agonized question I have ever asked I do not know the answer. I do not know why God would watch him fall. I do not know why God would watch me wounded. I cannot even guess.[1]

The lonely, the bereaved, the abandoned, the shunned, all these people are Unreconciled because they are aware of their capacity for connection and

---

1 Nicholas Woltersdorff, *Lament for a Son*, Grand Rapids: Eerdmans, 1997, pp. 67–8.

relationship and yet can make no progress with it. Quite often when some person shocks a community by going crazy with a weapon, like Michael Ryan in 1987, Thomas Hamilton in 1996 or Derrick Bird in June 2010, there is an attempt to 'explain' them as loners who had no real life among their peers.[1] Yet some of these people are quite capable of relationship but may find themselves profoundly lonely and cut off without anyone else realising their desperate state. When Raoul Moat murdered his former girlfriend's partner, injured his former girlfriend and blinded a police officer before taking his own life in July 2010, the Prime Minister suggested that it was inappropriate that a Facebook tribute be set up for him.[2] Tributes, the funerals, and the interrogation of events after the fact easily distract our attention from what was missing *before* the violence took place. We are less likely to ask ourselves whether things would have been different if we had taken a little bit more time to care about such people or taken more trouble to listen to them or to help them to belong. One of the best known quotations from the writer Bodie Thoene is: 'apathy is the glove into which evil slips its hand'.

All are called

What is humanity called to do then? Mission theology understands God as a missionary God, who not only sends the world into its being, but calls us to be co-creators in the matter of its transformation.

God does not call us to act randomly within a chaotic universe, just tinkering with bits of it, or tidying up the mess, rather, we are called to share in a vision of God's desire for the creation, a vision of worlds remade when the cycle of creation and destruction is at an end and everything is referential of God's faithfulness, wisdom and love. We don't have to wonder what that is supposed to be like. Scripture already offers us its vision:

> 'The wolf shall live with the lamb,
> The leopard shall lie down with the kid,
> The calf and the lion and the fatling together,
> And a little child shall lead them.
> The cow and the bear shall graze,
> Their young shall lie down together;
> And the lion shall eat straw like the ox.
> The nursing child shall play over the hole of the asp,
> And the weaned child shall put its hand on the adder's den.
> They will not hurt or destroy on all my holy mountain;
> For the earth will be full of the knowledge of the Lord
> As the waters cover the sea'
> Isaiah: 11.6–9

---

1 See for example: http://www.bbc.co.uk/news/10216923

2 Consider the comment at http://www.telegraph.co.uk/comment/columnists/ jennymccartney/7895985/Raoul-Moat-and-the-unacceptable-face-of-Facebook.html

This vision of peace with its end to fear and danger, life as purely a desperate struggle for survival, is the end of God's missionary desire and the inheritance of all those for whom God longs. The trouble is that many of us talk about the hope of eternal life with God and speak the words of the creed with its promise of Christ's return without necessarily owning that vision for ourselves or recognising our part in it. The Unreconciled often still live among and around us untouched by any part of the vision we jealously guard in our own safe little communities and congregations. Those people continue to live every day in fear and danger and in a constant struggle for survival. There is a *common* task for every single human being, called and disturbed by God, to recognise our own unreconciled natures and discover what God has done to heal them. Once we know that we are called to be reconciled to the image of God in us, then what God has done in Jesus begins to make sense and leads us into the mystery of the atonement. It is part of our obedience as God's people that we then share in a vision of reconciliation for all and agree with God that the creation is ultimately grace filled and intrinsically good. Christians have sometimes found this difficult to do, because our vision of the world is coloured or perhaps 'filtered' by sin and because of our need to express solidarity with those crushed by injustice. But unless we can see the world in which we find ourselves through God's eyes, we will not have a clear idea of our reconciling task or its ultimate purpose.

But what does God want with us? The answer to that question is hidden deep in the heart of the missionary enterprise and has to do with finding and recognising the Unreconciled and knowing that we are no different from them. In this, bringing new things to birth begins. Stories about how this has to happen are embedded in the history of God's chosen people. The book of Exodus relates how the people of Israel are led out of slavery in Egypt towards a vision of God's will for them in their own promised land, interpreted for them in the covenant at Sinai. Reconciliation for them is more than just liberation from slavery, occupying their own territory and finding peace; the 'land flowing with milk and honey' is also an eschatological vision, a dream of a restored Eden. Peace, prosperity and justice are properties of that vision and it is this the people must hold on to if they are to kindle the same flame of desire in the hearts of others around them, if they are to become a 'light to the nations'. Yet we know too, that the history of the people of Israel is characterised by pitfalls and lapses, so that the vision dims and dies. Through Scripture we hear the power of the prophetic voice urging that there is always the possibility of reconciliation between God and human beings and that such reconciliations are always marked by the promise of new birth, in powerful liberation and transformation:

> 'The spirit of the Lord is upon me
> Because the Lord has anointed me
> He has sent me to bring good news to the oppressed,

To bind up the brokenhearted,
To proclaim liberty to the captives,
And release to the prisoners;
To proclaim the year of the Lord's favour,
And the day of the vengeance of our God;
To comfort all who mourn
To provide for those who mourn in Zion –
To give them a garland instead of ashes,
The oil of gladness instead of mourning,
The mantle of praise instead of a faint spirit.
They will be called oaks of righteousness,
The planting of the Lord to display his glory.
They shall build up the ancient ruins,
They shall raise up the former devastations;
They shall repair the ruined cities,
The devastation of many generations.'

Isaiah 61.1–4

This is a profoundly missionary passage which combines the mission of the one who is sent by God with the acts of reconciliation. The environment of the Unreconciled, marked by ruin and devastation, mourning and despair, can be transformed by the coming of the good news. Such acts involve physical reconstruction, rebuilding, re-making the world, but also moral and spiritual regeneration, comforting and healing. Such acts allow the glory of the Lord to be seen clearly, and revealing that glory allows the vision to begin to become a reality.

It is not surprising then, that it is these words of Isaiah which Jesus reads from the scroll in his own local synagogue (Luke 4.18ff). It is here that he identifies with both the mission of God and with the acts of reconciliation which are needed to make that mission bear fruit. Therefore, Jesus' own ministry has a basis in acts of reconciliation which permit the larger vision of God's desire for all people to know and glorify him to be understood. So when Jesus heals people and forgives sin, this results not only in physical transformation, but also in a golden opportunity to realise the goodness and graciousness of God and respond to it. We are given the chance to respond to divine affirmation with our own 'Yes!' That is a choice that is given to the restored person, to share in their turn, what God has done for them in Jesus, or to go their own way, perhaps because they are not yet ready or equipped to do so, and not pursue the vision any longer. Jesus remarks on those that do this – and those that don't (Luke 17.11–19).

Such reconciliation forges powerful bonds between groups of Unreconciled in their estranged or segregated communities as in the parable of the Good Samaritan (Luke 10. 30–37) or in Jesus' conversation with the Samaritan woman at the well (John 4.1–42). God-fearing Jews did not associate with Samaritans. The Gospels also show that reconciling actions create bonds between 'clean' and 'unclean' people, between men and women, between adults and children, between the sick and the healthy, between the sinful and the righteous and the living and the dead. Everything that Jesus did in his ministry challenged such rifts and barriers and put in place the means for people to see that by small acts of reconciliation, the ultimate vision of the missionary God could be seen clearly and reached by everybody. No wonder the Pharisees hated him.

Glory

Jesus' ministry shows us why reconciliation is more than just healing a breach. With reconciliation comes opportunity, opportunity to cease scurrying around trying to stop things falling apart and to lift the veil to see God's glory and desire in a vision of perfection. Reconciliation within the mission of God comes complete with a window into eternity. Consequently, the tradition of the sacrament of reconciliation is so much more than confession and absolution; it is the provision of new possibilities, the renewal of God's call and confidence in us, without the burden of failure and regret.

> **'In the light of the Trinity, being a person in the image and likeness of the divine Persons means acting as a permanently active web of relationships: relating backwards and upwards to one's origin in the unfathomable mystery of the Father, relating**

Reconciliation Statue, Old Cathedral, Coventry, by Jim Linwood

outwards to one's fellow human beings by revealing oneself to them and welcoming the revelation of them in the mystery of the Son, relating inwards to the depth's of one's own personality in the mystery of the Spirit.'[1]

Our task then, is to remember the heavenly vision set before us and as St Paul gives it to us:

> 'From now on, therefore, we regard no one from a human point of view; even though we once knew Christ from a human point of view, we know him no longer in that way. So if anyone is in Christ, there is a new creation: everything old has passed away; see, everything has become new! All this is from God, who reconciled us to himself through Christ, and has given us the ministry of reconciliation; that is, in Christ God was reconciling the world to himself, not counting their trespasses against them, and entrusting the message of reconciliation to us. So we are ambassadors for Christ, since God is making his appeal through us; we entreat you on behalf of Christ, be reconciled to God. For our sake he made him to be sin who knew no sin, so that in him we might become the righteousness of God.'
>
> 2 Corinthians 5.16–21

The reconciling work of God, through Jesus' death on the cross, offers forgiveness and a new life with God that cuts through and abolishes the barrier of human sin. So, as Christians, we are called to share this news and make others aware of it, so that they too can forge new relationship with God. Similarly, whenever we demonstrate reconciling work, whether it is a large thing like supporting projects through the missionary societies, raising environmental awareness and helping with disaster relief, or in smaller things, like helping mend broken relationships, we are participating in God's mission and making the hope of heaven both more real and more near. The words of Revelation 21 are not just for the funeral service, but are about where mission and reconciliation are consummated: 'Then I saw a new heaven and a new earth; for the first heaven and the first earth had passed away and the sea was no more… And the one who was seated on the throne said, "see I am making all things new"'.

Because Jesus is raised from the dead, we can respond to God's invitation to be part of this missionary vision and ultimate enterprise for the beauty of creation, the creation that is 'good'. We can do this. We can make all things new.

---

1 Leonardo Boff, (1988) *Trinity and Society* (Maryknoll: Orbis) p. 149.

Speaking and Listening

Towards a methodology of reconciliation

If we are to reach the Unreconciled among us and to transform their situation, then it is clear that reconciliation requires a language, a set of symbols, a means of transaction which is powerful enough to overcome barriers, heal wounds, establish common ground and feed the creative process. Equally, we can be aware that there can be a language of the Unreconciled – that divides, hurts, wounds, and separates human beings from each other. This can include religious language. The symbolic story of how language divides human beings and drives them into confusion occurs in the story of the Tower of Babel (Genesis 11.1–9). The one language and unity of speech that connects human beings and God is lost when God 'confuses' sinful humanity and scatters them into different ethnic and language groups. This story is 'redeemed' by the Holy Spirit at Pentecost, where the gift is bestowed on the apostles of being able to be heard and understood by others from many other lands (Acts 2.1–11). The barriers to hearing and understanding are broken down by the transforming power of the Spirit. But while this is a powerful picture of God's reconciling work there are other matters to consider. Scripture indeed, while it contains transforming messages of love, inclusion, goodwill and joy, also includes the language of exclusion, confrontation and violent emotion. What models can we adopt that allow us to remove the speech that drives people into an Unreconciled state and which allow reconciliation to take place in an effective way?

Language as a tool of damage

> A young child was playing with his friends in the street. They played happily for a while, until the child cheated in a game they were playing. The other children began shouting and taunting the child: 'you're stupid', 'you're an idiot and so's your mum!' The child got on his bike and shouted back a phrase from the Catherine Tate Show, 'see this face? Do I look bovvered?' He then cycled round a corner, sat down and cried.

We all know the saying 'sticks and stone may break my bones but words will never hurt me' and know that it is untrue. Bullying is often a great deal less about physical threat or violence, than about emotional abuse through hurtful words and the spreading of malicious words. With the rise of the internet and mobile phone texting, hurtful language can be spread far and wide. The internet has provided new outlets for abusive communication,

and some children have been known to receive bullying and abusive text messages on their mobile phones. Adults can be hurt too. For example, Youtube[1] still carries news reports and images of Kevin Federline's face as he received a text message from the singer Britney Spears, telling him their marriage was over. It can hurt to be told, starkly, U R DMPD.

In Hanif Kureshi's novel *Intimacy*, the narrator, Jay, continues an interior monologue musing on his decision to leave his partner and their children and pursue another life of sexual freedom. The novel is perhaps unique in that it pursues a language which one reviewer said made it possible to sympathise with Jay but not to empathise with him. Jay acknowledges that his decision will hurt and scar his children, but he is unable to stop a stream of negative thoughts and ideas about his partner and the children, which have poisoned his existence and make the possibility of reconciliation beyond reach. It is a relationship in which love is not only impossible but eventually beyond imagining. He envies those who speak of and act in love, but cannot claim any of it for his own. The entire novel is a powerful description of the psychological state of some of the Unreconciled in our modern society, for Jay appears to live and work just like any other person, while he is entirely cut off from anything that will give him the meaning he craves. Even relationship counselling, intended to reconcile and heal the hurts, ends up for him as an even more painful process of humiliation and despair.

Listening

Reconciliation requires a commitment to dialogue and also to listening. The reparative and listening function of reconciling work, especially that done in conflict resolution, depends on the ability to give oneself over to the Other, to create empathy and to build on it. It is not an easy task. Techniques such

---

1 At February 2011.

as transactional analysis have revealed how easy it is for human beings to use language and listening to assume particular, even unconscious roles towards others, especially where there is difference and diversity among the speakers. Sociolinguistic studies also debate whether women's voices (for example) tend to be taken less seriously than men's in situations such as a courtroom or a committee meeting.[1]

> Isabel is a remarkable lady who has been a primary teacher for many years. What people remark most about her, is her ability to give a person her absolute attention. Someone talking to Isabel quickly comes to believe that they are the only person in the room. Isabel's attitude and body language indicate complete absorption in the actual task of listening and responding to the person; she sits in a composed stillness and waits for her interlocutor to 'unfold' as she puts it. Isabel says that her ability to pay attention to others comes from years of working with challenged children who may need time and space to interact with her. The task is first and foremost patience and waiting, without trying to rush the issue or force a conversation, or worse, simply put words into the child's mouth. Isabel also says that meditation and prayer enable her to assume the internal stillness required to create such attention and to put aside the demands of a busy schedule to enter the fascinating world of another person's mind and heart.

Listening is a particular art in a busy and noisy world. It requires the development of the facility of *attention,* so that we really feel that the story we tell is being absorbed and internalised by the Other. It is noticeable that in western society, people may turn to 'professional' listeners such as psychiatrists and psychotherapists. For such people, speaking and listening become a matter of therapy. This suggests that the mutuality and inter-dependence of speaking and listening are badly disturbed in our society and that we need the skills of others to put back what is wrong in our lives.

Gladys

In the old days I'd go to my doctor, even if I was fine and have a jolly good old chat. I'd tell him about things at home, and looking after my dad and about feeling down when my sister was in hospital. And he understood all that and he reassured me that I was ok, I could cope, that I was doing a good job. Nowadays you only get five minutes for an appointment, so you can't have a chat or even start. It's 'what's wrong with *you*?' But there's nothing wrong with *me*, it's the whole thing I want help with.

. . . .

---

1 An overview of the arguments and studies in this area can be found in Deborah Cameron (1985) *Feminism and Linguistic Theory,* (Basingstoke: Macmillan)

The inability to listen attentively and empathically to others has an effect on reconciling work. Reconciliation depends on the ability to build real relationships and these depend on the ability to listen, internalise and respond. Clearly certain sorts of language work better than others in building these relationships, but what should the characteristics of such language be? Is there a vocabulary for reconciliation, and if so, do we know how to use it?

Q (illegal immigrant working in a fish and chip shop)

This is ok, but I will have to move soon because the boss thinks I will get noticed. I am sorry because I have friends here. You're my friend. I speak good English now. I want to work and be with family. But the people (at a rival restaurant) tell on me. I would like to stay with all the friends and be accepted and do a good job of work. I can do books (accounting). I do not know what you mean (reconciliation) but I think it is being accepted, not chased after and abused. Being free with your friends. You are my friend. I give you cup of tea, milk, no sugar.

One way of looking at this is to look for models of divine Speech. There are several ways of examining this. In Scripture, God's speech among us can be made known to us through prophetic utterance; through divine messengers such as angels, through the words of Jesus during his life, and importantly, through the speech of the resurrected Jesus, a speech unique in human history. We can look at what each kind of speech or utterance contributes to reconciliation and how it breaks through into the world of the Unreconciled.

Prophetic speech

In Scripture, prophetic speech makes known God's thoughts or will towards human beings in a powerful and often dramatic way. Prophetic speech cuts through everyday human events, requiring people to think beyond the mundane and begin to ask questions about God. In the western world, where fashionable atheism often makes claims about human life and moral decisions, it is more important than ever to shape a prophetic language which recalls people to the promptings of God in their lives. We should be aware, however, that prophetic speech is not the language of the institution, and the Church, like any other institution, can be resistant to its rigorous truth. Walter Brueggemann, for example, warns that the institution of Church cannot bear the prophet's reality and can seek to undo it or to lessen its force.[1] Jesus himself ironically observed that a prophet is not acknowledged in his own country and among his own people. Prophetic speech is therefore also a speech from the margins and of the margins. We can discern the power (and unpopularity) of prophetic speech in some of the writings of liberation theologians and in the Minjung of Korea. Prophetic speech challenges the televangelists and prosperity gospels, it challenges bureaucratic systems of Church government, it cuts through the complacency of formulaic prayers and sermons. For example, these words of Archbishop Oscar Romero challenge the materialistic self-satisfied nature of western society, saying that the reconciliation offered by God at the Incarnation cannot come to people obsessed only with themselves:

> 'No one can celebrate a genuine Christmas without being truly poor. The self-sufficient, the proud, those who, because they have everything, look down on others, those who have no need even of God – for them there will be no Christmas. Only the poor, the hungry, those who need someone to come on their behalf, will have that someone. That someone is God, Emmanuel, God-with-us. Without poverty of spirit there can be no abundance of God'.[2]

Prophetic listening

We can also argue that there is such a thing as prophetic listening. Revelation 2.7 says: 'Let anyone who has an ear listen to what the Spirit is saying to the churches'. Listening for God's word requires a particular kind of discernment, and a willingness to turn aside from human debates about interim affairs and determine what God's Spirit is prompting from us. Even within the Church, speaking and listening can be overrun by particular theological

---

1 Walter Brueggemann (1978) *The Prophetic Imagination* (Minneapolis: Fortress Press).
2 Available from CAFOD at www.cafod.org.uk/worship/justice/panels/
 resources-to-download/quotes-from-romero.

positions or ideas leading to discord and disunity, and the prophetic listening required for a truly reconciling work simply may not happen.

Angelic speech

In Scripture the message of the angels represents a direct intervention from God's presence into human history. Angelic messages require human beings to react to the extraordinary within the ordinary and to be changed by it. The messages are both extraordinary and challenging and have the effect of transforming lives forever. The angel Gabriel, announcing the birth of Christ to the shepherds (Luke 2.8–20), offers peace and good will towards human beings, offers hope and change. This message comes to people who are *never* chosen to receive good news first. So such speech raises people like us and gives us identity, purpose and freedom. Angelic speech of this kind shows how certain kinds of language can penetrate to the heart of Unreconciled people and plant the seed of hope there.

Similarly, the angels at the empty tomb require human beings to think about the enormous possibilities of God's work (Luke 24.1–9). Such language guides human beings through mysteries which otherwise would be utterly bewildering and entirely terrifying. Angelic speech stands at the threshold between human action and God's own work, allowing reconciliation between human and divine worlds.

Jesus' teaching

In Scripture we encounter Jesus teaching others about God and calling them back to repentance. While much biblical scholarship is interested in what may or may not have been authentic sayings of Jesus, there are particular elements in Jesus-language which have implications for reconciling work.

First of all, Jesus tells parables – stories and illustrations which create mini-worlds in which God is always at work and can clearly be seen there by those who have eyes to see and ears to hear. The purpose of such story telling is to engage the imagination of the audience and ask them to make the mini-worlds their own then challenge them to put themselves into that virtual world, in the presence of God. This is something which we often fail to do in mission. We fail to create the idea of a Christian community for people in such a way that they can really imagine themselves a part of it, and even if we do, we often fail to *give* them the reality in a way that makes sense to them. Sometimes our church communities bear very little resemblance to the threshold of heaven and are full of people who have somehow missed the vision and forgotten to light their lamps.

The scriptural language that Jesus offers is also full of images of reconciliation. Stories of what is lost and found teach us about restoration of the order of things as they are meant to be (Luke 15). Jesus also offers us images of making new, including healing, transformation and establishing of joy. In entering these stories, the disciples, as new storytellers of God at work among human beings, are reconcilers. This does not mean rolling over or not issuing challenges; the path to reconciliation means dealing with obstacles, pressures and fractures in the human condition. Reconciliation requires repentance and forgiveness and these can fuel the missiological force of reconciling work. The use of parable and story telling is allied to our ability to play, wonder and dream, to explore and discover. This is a principle of the *Godly Play* process which seeks to engage children in an open ended exploration of Christian ideas and stories.[1]

Further, Jesus also speaks an intimate language of friendship, love and challenge to the disciples. This language is rooted in recognition, delight and powerful interest in their hearts and minds. Jesus goes out of his way to include his friends in his God-language, even when they cannot understand him, and includes in this intimacy even his own betrayer, for whom he has his own special language, itself a reconciling action: 'do quickly what you are going to do' (John 13.27). The other disciples, John says, do not know what this means.

Jesus also speaks words of command, using language which is meant to effect immediate transformation, the world restored to God's picture of it instantaneously. This is language that he uses in the act of healing: 'be opened', 'little girl, get up', 'be still'. In this way Jesus attests to the power of language to effect reconciliation, but which is dependent on perfect faith. Merely shouting louder will not do God's will, as the disciples find out when their attempts at healing fail and they discover they have not been able to release the Unreconciled people they want to help to change from their condition. In fact, their failure and appeal to Jesus to tell them why, means that they discover more about their *own* Unreconciled condition. Jesus says that the language that brings about transformation is the outward sign of true faith and which flows from it (Matthew 17.14–20).

The speech of the world to come

The New Testament also offers us a unique language, spoken by none other in the history of the world. This is the language of the resurrected Jesus. It is a gracious language, full of love and concern: 'come and have breakfast' 'peace be with you' 'feed my sheep'. It is a language which confirms God's promises. Death is silent. No more communication is possible. But Jesus' words to the disciples after his resurrection makes it clear that there is a language of heaven which binds the community of God's people together forever. How different then, this God-language is to the 'messages' offered by many psychics and mediums from the 'spirit-world' and how often we forget to point this out to those impressed by their claims and who come to believe that vague scraps of message are in fact the means to a reconcilia-tion. Hoodwinking those who live in the Unreconciled land of bereavement,

---

1 *Godly Play*, liturgically based materials for children, by Jerome Berryman, encourages exploration, wonder and dreaming about biblical themes. See www.godlyplay.org.uk

Nemi © Lise Myhre/distr. strandcomics.com

anxiety and grieving, by offering false visions or false hope, is a distressing side-effect of some of the more unscrupulous religious movements and DIY spiritualities in our society.

Giraffe and Jackal Language

Marshall Rosenberg has developed a theory of non-violent communication, in which he designates much of our typical discursive language as 'jackal' language.[1] Such language can be fundamentally aggressive, even if it is not intended as such, and often falls back on generalisations such as 'you always', 'you never…'. This sets up an internal dialogue in the other about the injustice of the generalisation, who thinks to him or herself 'I don't always…' 'It's not

1 Marshall Rosenberg (2nd edition 2003) *Nonviolent Communication: a Language of Life*, (Encinitas: Puddledancer Press). Also see the Center for Non-Violent Communication website at www.cnvc.org.

true that I never…'. and so the matter under discussion cannot proceed until this sense of injustice has been dealt with. In political debates, or discussions of policy issues, it is clear when one party has a good command of jackal when another person in the discussion begins to express disappointment or irritation at the picture being painted. Many politicians become experts in this kind of robust language in defence of their party's policies, avoiding damaging admissions and deflecting criticism back at opposing parties. Jackals impose a picture of the world on a situation and justify their actions in terms of this picture. Such language keeps the Unreconciled at arm's length, and confirms their status, challenging them to accept or shut up.

By contrast, as Philip Roderick explained to us, giraffes have 'soft ears and a big heart', so their language keeps options open and seeks to avoid the breakdowns caused by the internal dialogue about injustice. Counsellors, mediators and negotiators often learn specific forms of giraffe language to enable dialogue between warring parties or people in dispute. The trouble with giraffe language is that it can sound unnatural or even patronising. Continued phrases such as 'what did you just hear me say?' or 'what do you think I was saying?' can frustrate the listener and interfere with the process of dialogue. Some forms of everyday event are not conducive to giraffe language – Prime Minister's question time or university debates are not set up to permit giraffes to function effectively. Indeed, in the West, we live in a society where jackal skills can be useful – in interviews, in making claims, in oral exams, sales pitches and so on. The ability to silence the other through speech can be a good way of making a claim on the world and people are encouraged to learn these forms of discourse. TV programmes are also made about people whose aggressive violent language either makes or breaks people (eg The Apprentice, The F Word etc).

Notwithstanding, Christians often prefer to employ non-violent 'giraffe' communication in talking about public issues and are sometimes then misrepresented in the media. It is often harder for journalists to produce a story out of gracious, open-ended consideration than it is to deal with robust and aggressive statements. Discussion, debate, argument, and the rigorous language-statements of philosophy have all had their place in Christian apologetics and of course in the mission of the Church. More recently, however, there have been explorations of more giraffe-like communication in which people are encouraged to engage in and with story telling, wondering, dreaming, and exploration after the *Godly Play* model. It is a missionary task to examine the appropriateness of such languages in different contexts and to know what kind of approach best facilitates reconciliation. We have an example in the Jesus of the book of Revelation, whose kingship, glory and power is recognised not as domination but as the Lamb who has been slain from the foundation of the world.

Peace-languages

Peace-making, or any kind of reconciliation, can often be a delicate and difficult business. Peace-making is related also to justice, and to bringing about change in hearts and minds. Part of the problem can be determining the extent to which transformation has actually taken place, rather than a compromise or agreement which merely papers over the cracks.

In some forms of conflict resolution, where grievances have been held by unequal parties, there needs to be some mechanism by which the powerless or the marginalised can articulate what is wrong. For example, in the UK, where aggrieved parties have been disadvantaged because they cannot speak English sufficiently well, other communication methods in conflict resolution, such as drawing, working with textiles or role play have been employed to surmount the difficulties of trying to work with a foreign language.

Peace-languages for the establishment of justice can also be difficult to encourage in situations where there is tension. For example, following the Stephen Lawrence enquiry agencies have become very sensitive about all kinds of potentially offensive language, but in some cases, individuals can still carry divisive and hurtful ideas in their hearts and minds, whatever they might say in public. What has not been done in some of these situations is to accompany those whose organisations have been accused of institutional racism to try and find out where these attitudes and ideas have come from and what is happening in the course of their work to reinforce these attitudes. This is true in all kinds of communities where people are under duress, difficulty or living with tension. It is not enough to say that some sorts of language are unacceptable – reconciliation means getting to the pain in people's hearts which drives such language to the surface. *Big Brother* contestants have been censured or thrown out for unacceptable (especially racist) speech but while this may send one sort of signal it does nothing to drive out racism through reconciling actions and in the Shilpa Shetty racism debate it became important for people to feel that there was active reconciliation between the actress Shilpa Shetty and the late Jade Goody, particularly as the latter neared death. Rather, banning, fining or sacking people, such as in the fallout from the Jonathan Ross/Russell Brand obscene phone call affair, suggests that confirming people in an Unreconciled state (banishment, exile) is the way to solve such problems. This can also be true within the Church.

> A church group were praying for criminals and perpetrators. Having asked for God's mercy for all who have done wrong, an ensuing conversation turned to a local man who had murdered a schoolgirl. One lady turned to her friend and said 'may he rot in hell!' Everyone agreed.

There is also a difficulty with erasing the offensive language of the past, and some of it is part of the Church's heritage. For example, in Grahamstown,

South Africa, there are memorial stones which speak offensively about black people. Some students will not attend the church where these things are on the wall. What then is the right thing to do about such an inheritance? There has been a tendency to erase such language or stop people reading offensive language in books, but the problem with pretending it does not exist or can be exiled from people's consciousness, is that it teaches us nothing about change and transformation. That some form of language was acceptable then and is not acceptable now, tells us that we have learned something important enough to be transformative. It also gives us the opportunity to reflect on hurtful language and be sorry about it, and also to celebrate the change that has enabled us to realise it and transform our language into new forms of speaking and listening with one another.

Similarly, this means we can also address difficult language in the Bible without feeling that we should never use it in worship or just pretend it isn't there. For example, psalm 137 says 'Happy shall they be who take your little ones and dash them against the rock!' Such violent, murderous language is difficult to cope with, but wakes us up to the pain and mental anguish of the Unreconciled, in this case the Israelites who wept by the waters of Babylon.[1] Language which makes us recoil opens a window into the world of Unreconciled peoples and demands that we attend to their state. How can reconciliation take place if we ignore, hide from, or seek to cover up such speech even if it exists in our own tradition?

Inter faith dialogue
Another important form of reconciling language is that used in dialogues between religions. It is vitally important in times of heightened political tension and particularly when there is fear and worry about religious extremism that people of different faiths find ways to share and engage with each other. It is also vitally important that Christians engage in this process fully, especially as other religions may not have a concept of reconciliation exactly like that of the Christian tradition. Working together by hearing each other's faith stories and faith journeys and hearing about each others' Scriptures can help to lay foundations for transformation and for forming reconciled communities.[2]

> A church in a minority Christian area of the UK was finding it difficult to forge relationships with other faith communities around. The congregation set up a post box outside the church for prayer requests from the community and was astonished to find it filling up with requests from people of all faiths and ethnic backgrounds. The prayer post box enabled connections

1 See the chapter on Victimised and Victimisers, below.
2 There are excellent resources at http://www.presenceandengagement.org.uk including material for bible study.

to be made and relationships to be initiated, but the reconciling language was that of intercession.[1]

Liturgical language

Another important way in which reconciling language is spoken and owned by Christian communities is by the use of liturgical language in worship. Liturgical language, where words are spoken by the congregation in dialogue with a minister, or as a whole community of clergy and laity, enables feelings of solidarity and community to be built up. Christians, who may become over-familiar with texts, often fail to realise the power such language can have on newcomers or on people well outside the Church. Christmas services, baptisms, weddings and funerals, contain language that can stir people towards thoughts of what God might be saying in their lives. This is obviously an important reconciling mission opportunity, which can be missed by the familiarity which the words hold for Christians. This requires us to stop and look afresh at the power of the most well known phrases of our Christian liturgy.

'I am the resurrection and the life, says the Lord'

'In the beginning was the Word and the Word was with God and the Word was God'

---

1 Read more stories at http://www.presenceandengagement.org.uk/pdf_lib/66_resource. pdf.

We should also consider the range of our liturgical formats and recognise that different language forms can affect people in ways that don't affect us. For some people, Cranmer's language in the Book of Common Prayer may be essentially meaningless; for others, its poetry, rhythm and metre can offer them a glimpse of heaven. For many people, Latin is simply a dead language, yet for some young people, learning a hymn or using a Taizé chant in Latin can transport them to a sense of mystery, beauty and strangeness which they associate with the divine.

Obviously, this puts a burden on writers of liturgy and occasional services to remember what a missionary opportunity this is. Moreover, we should all be reminded periodically to reflect on what Christian liturgy may be offering to people who rarely, if at all, darken the doors of a church. Yet liturgical language can be the seed, nurture and birth of a new relationship with God. As Victoria Johnson says:

> '...our worship should echo that explosion of divine love exchanged between the persons of the Trinity. It should reflect, if only in part, the white heat of the Missio Dei which radiates out into the whole of the created order.
>
> ... The outworking of that reality is often a holy mess, but fortunately through the grace of the Holy Spirit working in the lives of those who come to worship, and in the life and the liturgies of the Church, this state of disorder can be fashioned into a creative and expressive assembly, where the disparate worshipping "I" is incorporated into one worshipping body, made up of many members.'[1]

People beyond the Church coming into the 'holy mess' can nonetheless be uplifted and find a powerful sense of connection to God:

> 'We have to allow for the possibility, that the pastoral offices, rites and rituals have within them, the potential to call people back into the liturgical life of the Church and begin, continue or deepen their journey of faith. These liturgies should also point to the possibility of further revelation, whether through scripture, other liturgies and sacraments, or through future life experience.'[2]

Music

In addition to the language used in Christian liturgy, there is no doubt that music also has power to create relationship and to heal rifts. This capacity of music is well known in all societies and is a powerful former of community. An advertisement for Nokia MP3 phones used this idea: a song will 'make

---

1 Victoria Johnson, (2008) 'Towards a Liturgical Missiology: A Trinitarian Framework for Worship, Mission and Pastoral Care' *Anaphora*, 2:2; see in context: pp. 33–44.
2 Ibid.

you call your ex', a song 'will make you call home' or 'will make you call a number you should have deleted long ago'. The message is simple: music reminds you of your most important relationships and makes you want to restore them to their perfect state. Singing together not only makes people feel themselves in community, but singing in harmony provides a living image of reconciled diversity. Many Christians are familiar with the round 'Father/Jesus/Spirit we adore you' sometimes used to illustrate the interweaving nature of the Triune God. Music enhances worship and makes it possible to glimpse the life of the heavenly community, which is characterised by adoration and praise. This the great church musicians and composers such as Tallis, Palestrina and J S Bach, and the great hymn writers such as Charles Wesley and Isaac Watts, knew very well.

In thinking about reconciliation, then, we should not overlook the power of music to effect reconciliation between people in community. Scientific research has been done on music therapy to see what effects music has on negative mood states, where it seems that music does really soothe the savage breast. The place of concerts, music evenings, dances, children's choral events, carol singing and 'Messiahs from scratch' have an important place in local communities. Nor should anyone interested in mission forget the place of contemporary music in people's lives and look closely at the kind of music people choose for the occasional offices. Where are people receiving spiritual nourishment through music, and what do we make of those modern groups and music styles which deliberately use religious vocabulary? And if we are quick to judge the quality of modern music these days as it is swapped, downloaded and sold to us on memory sticks, could we be overlooking what is in fact a powerful reconciling force which is binding a generation together and reaching deep into the heart of groups of Unreconciled?

Lies and Truth

Bearing witness among the Unreconciled

Language can be an agent of reconciliation, a life giving, life affirming tool, but it is also a primary tool of evil and one which both creates and sustains the communities of the Unreconciled. The serpent in the Garden of Evil plants the seed of disobedience in Eve's head by telling her a different story, in language which works on her will and her imagination (Genesis 3.1–5). Once untruth and manipulation of the truth become established they create their own alternative reality, so that the clear communication between human beings and God gets twisted and damaged. So reconciliation for mission means addressing the language of lies and deception which condemns some groups of Unreconciled people to their state and also means learning to recognise and understand how lies come into the world and how they work.

The neurologist Oliver Sacks tells the story of a group of people whose brain damage made them unable to understand spoken language any longer. He was puzzled by watching a group of them watching an American president talking on the television and laughing at him, although the speech was very sincere and earnest. On enquiry he discovered that the group were able to tell from the man's tone the falsity of what he was saying.[1]

Scripture is clear about the terrible harm that lying and dissembling can do to human relationships. Indeed, God's word to humankind, enshrined in the Ten Commandments, is not to bear false witness. The story of Susanna,[2] where a virtuous woman stands to lose her life because of the lies of powerful men with evil in their hearts, tells us how wisdom must be employed to determine the truth of any situation. In the story of Susanna, discrepancies in the evidence given by her accusers demonstrate that her version is correct and her accusers tied up in their fabrications. Similarly the famous story about the Judgement of Solomon (1 Kings 3. 16–28) has a situation in which Solomon must determine which of two women is telling the truth about being the mother of a child. Solomon offers to divide the child in half, thus killing it. Love reveals the truth, overcoming the dominant and overbearing speech of the lie.

Pilate asked Jesus 'what is truth?' (John 18.38) and so the issue of reconciliation in mission must deal with the complex issue of truth telling. In this sense reconciliation is powerfully wedded to mission, since mission

---

1 Oliver Sacks, (1985) *The Man Who Mistook His Wife for a Hat* (London: Picador 1986 edition) chapter 9, 'The President's Speech'.
2 One of the apocryphal books, being chapter 13 of the Greek version of Daniel.

is about offering 'truth' to people, the truth of what God has done in Jesus and the truth which people may adopt for themselves as a story by which to live. But similarly, reconciliation means the shedding and exposure of lies, which includes the propagation of particular kinds of story and particular kinds of history.

Israel Selvanayagam also adds this warning about the easy acceptance of truth:

> Accepting the truth of Jesus and all he revealed should not be an easy way or a shortcut for Christians. Accepting Jesus as one's personal Lord and Saviour means being subjected to the reign of someone crucified and risen, the Lion-turned-Lamb, having all authority yet bleeding, and to participate in his saving process as portrayed, for example, in the Book of Revelation. Christians are called to share this vision not with a 'crusading mind' but a 'cruci-fied mind', to use the wise words of Kosuke Koyama. Christians,

then, have a long way to go to realise fully the cost of disciple-
ship while being healed as well as healing, a witnessing church
needing to be reconciled as well as reconciling. Truth shines out
when believers are humble enough to distinguish between what
they know and what they have yet to know, between what they
are and what they have yet to be. When Christian believers accept
this orientation to a new future, other believers may likewise be
inspired to do so. Then, together, they can witness to the truth
of reconciliation and the reconciliation of truth. Then they can
move towards the future with serious commitment and honest
openness. [1]

Mikaela (community liaison)

My job is all to do with reconciliation. Cos people round here have strong views
about asylum seekers and refugees. You get people here who have been poor all
their lives, they've had a struggle and they still feel they're always scrapping for
what they can get. They don't mind if everyone is in the same boat and has the
same history, but when asylum families and refugees end up being housed on
the same street, it starts resentment and anger. They don't want to know what
the story is. Sometimes the stories are too weird to get their head round. So I'm
trying to get people a hearing, get people to talk to each other and help each
other. You come up against such harsh words: 'pigs in our trough', but I still
think people are basically kind and helpful and even if they say and act tough,
they'll help out if they can. Reconciliation depends on people actually learning
each other's stories (it works both ways) and that can be difficult when the
asylum seekers are traumatised or don't want to share or aren't interested in

1 *Truth and Reconciliation – An Interfaith Perspective from India* presented in a conference at
  St John's York 2006 and published in Sebastian Kim, Pauline Kollontai and Greg Hoyland
  (eds) (2008) *Peace and Reconciliation: in search of shared identity*, (Farnham: Ashgate).

their neighbours and want to keep themselves to themselves. You get problems with money being spent on services and provision 'just for them' like places for worship and the books and information in foreign languages. It all gets seen as special privilege. Reconciliation means getting beyond all that and offering life to people in need.

. . . .

The TRC

For this reason, the Truth and Reconciliation Commission in South Africa after apartheid has included both the telling of a truth which has never been able to be told and also the exposure and confirmation of lies. The commission has enabled the stories of those groups of Unreconciled people who had no voice and no power to be told and for those stories to become the agents of healing as well as the foundations for a new beginning.

> Piet Meiring tells of hearing a woman tell her story of what happened to her son during apartheid. The details were so shocking and harrowing, he wondered if getting her to relive the experience was really the best way to achieve reconciliation. He asked her afterwards if it hadn't been all too much for her. She told him that the night to come would be the first night in nine years when she would be able to sleep. Although the story was terrible, the emergence of truth over the lies would allow her to rest and move on.

Facing the truth is difficult, but has the power to liberate and to sustain. More important than this though, is the observation that such truth needs to be spoken, heard and witnessed in a context which includes God.

> Piet Meiring tells the story of Archbishop Desmond Tutu being asked to preside over a TRC hearing. He was warned, however, that he should not preside in his clergy role and that there would be no need for prayer or praise. He should just get on with the business. So Archbishop Tutu opened the proceedings and then stopped. The witnesses came in, but still he did nothing. People became embarrassed as he shuffled his papers and fidgeted. Eventually, he seemed to come to a decision and said that it was impossible to go on without prayer and inviting God to be part of the proceedings and went ahead with prayer and hymn singing. As soon as this happened, the atmosphere changed, people relaxed and the business of hearing terrible stories was able to continue. It simply could not be done outside the context of God as witness.

The history of the Church and the history of missions has been one of different and sometimes contradictory truths. Missiology then needs to have a constant reparative dialogue with historical and ecclesiological truth. This goes back to the idea of offering a story of truth to others and allowing them to make it their own and reflect it back to us in a way that changes us. To do otherwise, to colonise people's heads, or to impose Christian ideas and values on people who cannot accept them is itself as form of lying, what Robert Schreiter calls 'the narrative of the lie'. [1] People who are thus bludgeoned into faith remain Unreconciled and need to be helped to find their own truth. It is difficult to know, for example, whether if we insisted, as in the story above, on including God in external affairs, this would be interpreted by our own society as an attempt to assert Christian domination.

Christian witness

Another form of truth telling involves Christian witness. 2 Corinthians refers to Christians as letters from God (2 Corinthians 3.2–3). So Christian witness requires us to represent those missives as Christ has written them upon us. We human beings, however, tend to rewrite such letters to our own liking and style, to try and improve on them, emphasise some sections over others. Such rewriting in the course of human witness leads to distortion of God's truth and the ability or even necessity to use portions of it to treat others badly. Effectively, and sometimes with the best will in the world, we rub out God's signature and write our own.

We also sometimes naively assume that truth telling is the only way to achieve reconciliation. But Ecclesiastes 3.7 warns us that there are times to speak and times to refrain from speaking. Revealing the whole truth is not always appropriate and can do harm to vulnerable people condemning them to be Unreconciled. Archbishop Rowan Williams says:

> Since the Fall concealment is necessary and good in the sense that there is plenty in human thought, feeling, and experience that should not be part of shared discourse. We are alienated, divided, and corrupted; but to bring this into speech (and to assume we thereby tell better or for the truth) is to collude with sin.[2]

Truth telling can be cynically used as a destructive weapon or tool, it then becomes a lie. Concealing truth for the sake of preserving life can sometimes be of greater moral value than telling the truth. The critical issue in reconciliation is not whether we know all the truth but what we do with the truth that has been uncovered. Truth only becomes truth for us when we interact with it and are changed by it.

Contexts for truth

Another aspect of truth telling is that an appropriate context has to be established within which the truth can be told. There can be no true reconciliation between a strong person and a weaker person. Without equality,

---

1 In (1992) *Reconciliation: Mission and Ministry in a Changing Social Order*, (Maryknoll, NY: Orbis).

2 Rowan Williams, (1988) 'The Suspicion of Suspicion: Wittgenstein and Bonhoeffer' in Richard H Bell (ed) *The Grammar of the Heart* (San Francisco: Harper and Row), p. 44.

the Unreconciled have no foundation on which to change their status. True reconciliation can only be among equals. The South African Council of churches in 1968 said that it was impossible to talk about reconciliation while apartheid still existed. There must be equality of partners before reconciliation can happen. This is something that Christians do not always think about when examining the relation between mission and social justice. The poor and needy must be raised up because speaking on their behalf risks entrenching them in their silent state. Speaking on behalf of those whose voices need to be heard is a transitional state which is on the road to reconciliation but cannot represent reconciliation itself. The voice-less and powerless must be given voices and so empowered. We have to hear the truth of the Unreconciled and accept the indictment it carries, not circumvent the unpalatable truth with the polished voice of our own. In the book of Job, he says to his comforters with considerable irony:

> **'How you have helped one who has no power!**
> **How you have assisted the arm that has no strength!**
> **How you have counselled one who has no wisdom, and given**
> **much good advice! With whose help have you uttered words and**
> **whose spirit has come forth from you?'**
> Job 26. 2–4

By talking at him and without making sense of what has happened to him, Job's comforters can offer him no truth and bring nothing new to birth. Job knows that he remains in the world of the Unreconciled. His comforters would turn him into a victim, but Job knows that although he may have been victimised there is more to his state than being a mere 'worm' as his comforters suggest. This distinction between the victimised and the state of victim will be considered in the next chapter.

Victimised and Victimisers

What is Victimhood?

Unreconciled people who experience the evil of the world in terrible ways are often described as 'victims', but what kinds of assumptions come with this word and is it really an appropriate word to use? Bishop Brian Castle, for example, writes that while it could be argued we are all victims at one time or another and it is a state which we experience as an inevitable part of human life, being a victim lessens our humanity and prevents reconciliation. These experiences of victimhood help us to recognise the Unreconciled state of being.

> '...it could be argued that victimhood is a state shared by everybody: regardless of how self-aware and liberated a person may be, all people are victims of some circumstance or other at some level in their lives.'[1]

Such victimhood is typically associated with a powerlessness which condemns that person to a particular world of the Unreconciled without hope of escape.[2] We would say that a victim is one who cannot withstand the evil visited upon her. Or we would say that a victim of famine has no means of acquiring food; a victim of AIDS has no immunological defences against disease; a victim of abuse has no means of escape from the perpetrator. However, as Brian Castle argues, there needs to be a distinction between being a victim and being victimised. Jesus was victimised, but he was not a victim in the way that victimhood is understood in the twenty-first century. Being 'victimised' carries the sense of the unequal power relations which contribute to the Unreconciled state and contain a hint of what must happen to change things for the better. How people behave in relation to being victimised then makes a difference to their hopes for reconciliation. A victimised person need not necessarily accept the shackles of victimhood. Reconciliation for victimised people can mean helping them to reclaim power and autonomy and so to escape from the powerlessness that made them 'victims' in the first place.

Understanding how this works also has important implications for mission. For example, research done by Deenabandhu Manchala and Peniel Rajkumar for the Edinburgh 2010 World Mission Conference on 'Foundations for Mission', focused on the experience of Indian Dalits (Untouchables),

---

1 Brian Castle, (2008) *Reconciling One and All, God's Gift to the World*, (London: SPCK) p. 31.
2 *Ibid.*

Photographs of those killed (except for 92 victims and terrorists onboard the flights) during the terrorists attacks on 9/11.

found that the Dalits' conversion to Christianity also gave birth to something new – an experience of liberation from the condition of victim, both in terms of social status and in terms of their new Christian life, which they needed to embrace for themselves, rather than have it imposed upon them:

> 'Dalit communities, which had no stake in local power, viewed those in their own country who had power as 'colonizers'. For them, the conversion experience of which they were the primary agents helped in their quest for freedom from oppression. In this the conditions of mission played and continue to play the role of midwife. Hence proclamation, pastoral care and social justice are all recognised as part of the mission of God. The agency for this mission extends beyond the church.'[1]

Empowerment and reconciliation

Therefore, in the missiological view of reconciliation it is not enough to feed a hungry person. Reconciling action would mean empowering that person to grow or otherwise obtain their own food, not remain dependent

---

1 Daryl Balia and Kirsteen Kim, (eds) (2010) *Edinburgh 2010: Witnessing to Christ Today*, Volume 2, (Oxford: Regnum Books) p. 15.

on the goodwill or handouts of others. People need to be given back their autonomy and sense of self-responsibility, the ability to make decisions and speak for themselves and to recover purpose and self esteem. In this way those Unreconciled who have been victimised by poverty or famine can become again part of what Raymond Fung called 'The Isaiah Vision' based on Isaiah 65.20 23 which he says states clearly God's desire for autonomy and self-reliance, specifying:

> '-that children do not die;
> -that old people live in dignity;
> -that those who build houses live in them;
> -and those who plant vineyards eat the fruit.'[1]

Responding to need, perhaps by giving to a charity after moving pictures of suffering people have appeared on the television is only the beginning of a process that assures the victimised person moves out of victim status for ever and becomes truly free. The reconciliation of such people requires facing the evil that victimises them, and dealing with that issue on both a short term and long term basis to move everyone involved to a place where that evil can no longer cause harm. There is memory which informs the future and also learning, which moves us further towards the Kingdom. This too is part of mission and insists that mission be the major informer at the heart of social justice, the *why* of social action.

For example, at a conference in Rio, a group of theologians made the point that in the story Jesus told about the Good Samaritan (Luke 10.30–37), we do not always think about the wider context of the story. The road where the man was ambushed was a very dangerous road, and *stayed* a very dangerous road. So what has to happen for the impact of the Samaritan's good works to have an effect on the danger and violence of that road for everyone? Jesus is clear: everybody has to recognise that each human person is our neighbour. We all have to care, despite our differences, problems and weaknesses. The Isaiah vision cannot be realised until everyone who walks the road is dedicated to keeping all who use it safe from harm.

'The story of Good Samaritan can be read as a critique of the Church, represented by the Priest and Levi, walking around a victim of violence. Here, the stranger and even the innkeeper were more just than the representatives of the institutional church. Those who were called to be the keepers of healing, peace and justice walked and passed by the victim and left the system of oppression intact. The road to Jericho becomes the context of the system and the structures that create victims of violence. Does the road to Jericho become safer because of the Good Samaritan? It will continue to be treacherous until the challenge to injustice becomes the norm. Some do not respond out of fear, some do not respond because they have other things to

---

1 Raymond Fung, (1992) *The Isaiah Vision: an ecumenical strategy for congregational evangelism*, (Geneva: WCC Publications) p. 2.

do and it is not a priority, some are the beneficiaries of injustice and violence, some do not notice, and some do not want to get their hands dirty.

The road is different for each person who goes down the road. Each person is connected differently to the road. How does the victim of violence perceive those who are walking away and around him? She is helpless, out of control of the situation, and needs to be helped, to be healed, and bandaged. The system or those around her are responsible for the healing and bringing of justice. But it does not stop there; the road needs to be made safe for the next person with vulnerability and it is the responsibility of the system to make the road safe. Once the victim is healed, bandaged and able to walk again she must also now be part of the responsibility to make the road safe by speaking out and being a witness.'[1]

1 WCC (2009) 'Re-visioning justice from the margins of the new world of 21st century', report of a continuing conversation among theologians representing the concerns of people living with disabilities, Indigenous Peoples, Dalits and those struggling against racism, on churches becoming and effecting just and inclusive communities at Colégio Assunção, Rio de Janeiro, Brazil 18–23 August 2008. Online at: http://www.oikoumene.org/en/resources/documents/wcc-programmes/unity-mission-evangelism-and-spirituality/just-and-inclusive-communities/rio-report-re-visioning-justice-from-the-margins.html.

Is a *dead* person a victim forever?

The wounded man in the story of the Good Samaritan was saved and healed, but it could be argued that a person who is dead is truly a victim because he is ultimately powerless and incapable of doing anything else to change his state. However, in Genesis 4.8–10, when Abel is killed, God says to Cain, his murderer, that Abel's blood cries from the ground. The dead person was a completely unique individual and is now lost to the human community but he is still part of a family and a community which is similarly victimised by the evil perpetrated and those left behind can still act and react. When a person is murdered, justice and reconciliation must work together to heal the damage which involves so many more people than the murdered person.

In Albert Camus' *The Plague*, an allegory of occupation by the Nazis in the Second World War, the priest and the doctor of the afflicted town take different views of the way the plague takes its victims. The priest first argues that the townspeople must have deserved their affliction and hence their victimhood, by not paying enough attention to God. The doctor disagrees, and when a little child suffers horribly and dies, the priest does not know how to explain his death and the impact on his family. But this in itself brings vastly different people together to work against the victimising evil: those indifferent to the town's fate, the timid, the arrogant, the pessimistic and the altruistic. As the doctor Rieux says to Paneloux, the priest, 'God himself cannot part us now'. The dead person energises reconciling work in others to resist evil and bring healing to the damaged community.

Children's section of Camargo graveyard, by Tomas Castelazo.

As far as the dead person is concerned however, there is a distinction between a view in the Hebrew Scriptures that a dead person like Abel remains a victim crying out for justice and a New Testament view that victimhood ends with death because a dead person is alive in God. So unavenged death in the Hebrew Scriptures can lead to an Unreconciled state of trapped victimhood for the lost person and those left behind within the community. Yet the community realised that unrestrained retaliatory violence is not the answer to the Unreconciled state. The *lex talionis* (eye for an eye principle – see Exodus 21.23) was not a licence to violent redress, but a restriction on the extent of retribution. Jesus however, implies that even living by these restrictions could not justify violence; a right heart is needed with which to love enemies and pray for those that persecute you. (Matthew 5.38–39).[1]

Further, in Christ, death becomes a gate to a life without victimhood, a freedom from the destructive forces of the world. This is demonstrated in those people whom Jesus raises from the dead. Though disease takes Lazarus (John 11.38–44), the widow of Nain's son (Luke 7.11–17) and Jairus' daughter (Luke 8.49–56), devastating their families, yet Jesus calls them forth, whole, restoring them to their loved ones and bringing into their communities the understanding that beyond the grave there is an ultimate reconciliation where victimhood is no more. Jesus' command that Lazarus should be 'unbound' and set free provides an image of this reconciling liberation from being a victim.

People who are trapped or who need to be victims

There are also victimised persons who can become trapped in the Unreconciled world of those claiming status as victims and who then become unreachable. In some cases the wronged person can also become the oppressor, not the oppressed one. A 'victim' can also be someone who remains enslaved in a relationship to the oppressor. That person may need to remain there; it may be more comfortable to stay in that dark place rather than move out into the light.[2] Other people like to feel they are victims and use that idea as a blanket to get attention or sympathy from others, without being able to contribute back to the community or help their families: 'the very discourse of "victimization" has become a commodity by which people attempt to purchase compassion'.[3] Giving up victimhood and the special status it can confer can itself be traumatic and difficult to release. Can one who insists on their victimhood be reconciled? Reconciliation must happen

---

1 For more on this see John Pratt (2008) 'Retribution and Retaliation' in S Giora Shoham, Ori Beck and Martin Kett (eds), *International Handbook of Penology and Criminal Justice* (Boca Raton, Florida: CRC Press) p. 395.

2 In the film *The Shawshank Redemption* the prisoner Brooks commits suicide rather than face liberation from prison. The prospect of freedom after years of incarceration is more than he can bear.

3 L Gregory Jones (1995), *Embodying Forgiveness, a Theological Analysis*, (Grand Rapids, Michigan: Eerdmans) p. 46.

between equals – and the victimised person may not want equality or to be reconciled. For some, the landscape of this group of the Unreconciled is the only familiar place and the idea of forging new connections or reclaiming old ones too painful or too frightening. Reconciliation means entering into the challenge offered by people defining themselves as victims and finding ways to allow them to move on. This is again a missiological process because the release of the victimised into true personhood is part of the stated mandate of the *missio dei* (Luke 4.18/Isaiah 61.1) and this movement towards wholeness and healing is blessed by God.

Beyond those people who want to cling to their self-definition of victims, we must distinguish those people who remain trapped unwillingly in their victimhood, even though the evil which has hurt them has passed. For some, the trauma of their experience has invaded their psychological space and becomes defining for them. So some men and women who have experienced torture, rape or other extreme violence, such as in war, end up confined to their houses or safe places, unable to interact with the world, avoiding people, places and things which remind them of the event, perhaps even unable to speak or make sense of their surroundings. A whole range of deeply debilitating symptoms of this kind are often seen in post-traumatic stress disorder. Such people need medical help and support to emerge from this frightening and disabling place. Often, however, other people find it difficult to understand what PTSD does to a person's experience of life and urge people who appear physically well to 'get over it' 'pull yourself together' or 'move on', when it is impossible for them to do so without help.

Wendy

I was in the car with my boyfriend and he was driving too fast. I begged him to stop but he wouldn't. He was showing off to his mate in the passenger seat. Showing off and showing off, you know? I was really frightened. I don't remember much about the accident. They told me that he tried to overtake a lorry and ran out of road. There were three lanes and then two. They told me the car hit the lorry and spun into the middle bit, you know, the barrier, and turned over. I was badly injured and my boyfriend and his mate were killed.

When I left hospital I had nightmares about the crash even though I couldn't remember it. I can't get in a car any more I just start shaking and crying. I can't go near the road where it happened. I don't know what has to happen to make me feel better. I've got pills and things. I'm so angry with my boyfriend and I'm angry with myself for not being stronger and making him slow down. I think his family blames me even though they say they don't. I wish I could sleep. It's just there like a big monster. It's there every day. I can't think about whether there will ever be some time, some moment, when it will be in the past, something that happened. It's all of my life, every day.

Atrocity and genocide

Another matter we have to confront in exploring the world of the Unreconciled among victimised and victimisers is how we approach the issue of genocide and the human capacity to perform atrocities. The sheer number of people who have lost their lives in history, especially perhaps during the wars of the 20th century, challenges everything we think we know about victimisers and victimised and sharpens our responsibility to nourish the Unreconciled survivors into liberated life. These people, human beings like ourselves, have wounds in their psyche which we cannot imagine if we have not experienced it ourselves. This means that events in the Middle East, whether we are talking about reconciliation between Palestinians and Jews, or hoping for a cessation of the suicide bombings in Iraq, require so much more than political solutions. Where people have survived an attempted genocide, whether in Europe, Africa, or the Middle East, it can create a sense for people that no matter how powerful, successful and strong they later become, no matter how faithful or religious, they are forever condemned to facelessness, loss of identity, lack of recognition and the desire in others, never stated, but always there, to exterminate them. And sometimes this is exactly what such people hear. To believe that your fellow human beings resent your very existence and wish you gone is powerfully disabling, even in a position of strength, and can fuel intense, irrational anger and despair; it drives an exodus into a community of Unreconciled people who have nothing more to lose.

For Christians, then, responding to the pain of those who have experienced unimaginable atrocity and genocide is a complex and heart searching business that is not served by traditional forms of mission and evangelism, but by a reconciling solidarity which asks our fellows to reach deep into their shattered hearts for images of neighbour to explore with those others. Moreover, we cannot expect such reconciliation to come quickly or easily, but be prepared for long years of gradual exploration and letting go of the ghosts of the victimised who still cry in the psyche of such people for justice. For the purposes of reconciliation we must distinguish between those who are victimised and those who are wronged. Those who are wronged can see a path to restitution and justice, but those who are victimised may be unable to deal with ideas of justice. We cannot then, deal with these groups of the Unreconciled as a set of wronged individuals, but as people trapped by a victimhood that has become part of their tradition and significant memory, a 'chosen trauma'.[1]

People who refuse to be victims

Conversely some people, whom society sometimes casts as victims, refuse to be so classified. Many people with disabilities would refuse the 'victim' label.

---

1 See Vamik Volkan ((2006). *Killing in the Name of Identity: A Study of Bloody Conflicts* (Charlottesville, VA: Pitchstone Publishing)

For example, many deaf people feel that the hearing community should not offer 'treatment' to allow them to speak, because of the richness and variety of their own signed culture, which more than compensates for what hearing people might consider a deficit. If we designate deaf people as Unreconciled to our hearing world, they would dispute the need to be reconciled to the hearing world in the first place. We can learn from such cultures wherever we find them.

Similarly, there are many others who are victimised by unjust structures of society who, while suffering oppression and damage, also refuse their victimhood and embrace ideological, political and indeed spiritual struggle:

> **'One day, one day I was goin' to pray**
> **Thank God A'mighty I'm free at las'**
> **I met ole Satan on my way**
> **Thank God A'mighty I'm free at las'**
> **Whut you reckon, whut you reckon ole Satan had to say?**
> **Thank God A'mighty I'm free at las'**
>
> **Young man, young man, you's too young to pray**
> **Thank God A'mighty I'm free at las'**
> **Ef I'm too young to pray, I ain't too young ter die**
> **Thank God A'mighty I'm free at las'** [1]

The slaves on the plantations, often *refused* to be victims; in their spirituals, like the one above, they sang about being liberated.[2] They created imaginary worlds in which they could inhabit their liberation, even while they were still chained (cf 2 Corinthians 4:7–15). Indeed, they were already liberated on one level; they just needed their owners to hear it.

The term 'survivance' has also been used of the indigenous Indian peoples of North America to refer to their determination to hold on to their sense of community, language and culture despite their treatment by the dominant culture. Survivance is seen 'in native stories, in natural reason, remembrance, traditions and customs and is clearly observable in narrative resistance, and personal attributes, such as the native humanistic tease, vital irony, spirit, cast of mind and moral courage. The character of survivance creates a sense of narrative presence over absence, nihility, and victimry.'[3]

The same determination was also seen in South Africa during apartheid. Despite crushing injustice, people were capable of refusing their victimhood created by apartheid; they needed apartheid to be removed for them fully to

---

1 Federal Writers Project, South Carolina, (1937) *Twenty-One Negro Spirituals*, (New York: Viking Press) online at http://newdeal.feri.org/texts/612.htm

2 Also see Brian Castle, op. cit., pp. 41–3.

3 Gerald Vizenor, (ed) (2008) *Survivance: Narratives of Native Presence*, (Lincoln, NE: University of Nebraska Press) p.1.

be able to inhabit that liberation and begin a process of establishing equal power relations with their victimisers. This process is not achieved by single events such as the removal of apartheid, the establishing of the TRC, or the freeing of Nelson Mandela, but marks a journey in which these events move the process forward and raise consciousness about what it means to be free in South Africa. So, for example, during the 2010 World Cup in South Africa, the suggestion that vuvuzelas (plastic trumpets) be banned from games because they were too noisy, led to protests that the vuvuzela is part of South African culture, exuberance and football experience which should not be suppressed.

In her book *What it means to be Palestinian*, Dina Matar interviewed eighty people about their experiences, and these show that today, in Palestine, many people living there feel that they must refuse to accept the status of victims no matter how victimised they might be. If they adopt the category of victims, then Israel has won. This is summed up by her interview with an artist who said 'The Israelis thought we would come out of prison like rotten tomatoes but we came out as apples' and another spoke of his time away from Palestine in exile: 'now that I am an old man and more reflective I can tell you that my experiences taught me that you can survive anything. You can survive loss but not non-belonging'.[1]

The Victimised in Exile

In these kinds of situations, the world of the Unreconciled, victimised by slavery and apartheid, was set in a context that can be viewed with the hindsight of history as a time of exile. Scripture gives us models for this in the history of Israel and the response to the prophetic voice to exile and feelings of abandonment, especially as the people of Israel tried to make sense of the Babylonian captivity:

> 'By the waters of Babylon – there we sat down and there we wept
> when we remembered Zion.
> On the willows there we hung up our harps.
> For there our captors asked us for songs,
> And our tormentors asked for mirth, saying,
> "Sing us one of the songs of Zion!"
> How could we sing the Lord's song in a foreign land?'
> Psalm 137.1–4

In this psalm the people of Israel exiled from their homes and in captivity, weep for what they have lost. They have a choice. They can succumb entirely, beaten and broken, or they can refuse to be victims by finding hope through continued faith in God. The psalm continues:

---

1 Dina Matar (2010) *What it means to be Palestinian, Stories of Palestinian Peoplehood,* (London: I.B.Tauris). Extract was quoted at www.suite101.com in a review article prior to publication.

'If I forget you, O Jerusalem, let my right hand wither!
Let my tongue cling to the roof of my mouth, if I do not remember
you,
If I do not set Jerusalem above my highest joy.' (v.6)

The people refuse to be victims by steeping themselves in memory and renewed vision. By holding on to faith in God and to a vision of a restored community, they retain their identity and refuse the status of victimhood. Yet we cannot pretend that this solves all problems and leads to reconciliation, restoration, justice and peace. The ending of Psalm 137 as we noted above is one of the more shocking and violent passages in Scripture as the psalmist dreams of violent revenge and killing Babylonian children as payback for the sufferings of Israel. The emergence from victimhood can all too easily spill over into becoming a victimiser in turn, exacting revenge and payback and perpetuating the world of the Unreconciled. René Girard, writing in *Things Hidden since the Foundations of the World*, shows that religious communities have often entered this unremitting cycle of suffering and revenge: in refusing to be victims we must emerge into something new, not simply copy our oppressors and become what we hate.[1] As Walter Wink says:

'The very act of hating something draws it to us. Since our hate is usually a direct response to an evil done to us, our hate almost invariably causes us to respond in the terms already laid down by the enemy. Unaware of what is happening, we turn into the very thing we oppose'.[2]

How then, do we get out of this Unreconciled condition? For Christians, the answer lies in work and words of Jesus, teaching us how to live and giving us a permanent way out through his Cross and Resurrection. The question is, do we *really* know how to live as he intended us to, or are we still stuck in our victimiser/victimised roles?

Jesus as reconciler among the victimisers and the victimised
Both Girard and Wink turn to Jesus as a way of seeing someone who was able to break out of the cycle of damage and revenge, giving human beings tools for peace-making and reconciliation. Girard says:

'The decision to adopt non-violence is not a commitment that he (Jesus) could revoke, a contract whose clauses need only be observed to the extent that the other contracting parties observe them…Despite the fact that all the others fall away, Jesus continues to see himself as being bound by the promise of the Kingdom. For him, the word that comes from God, the word that enjoins us to imitate no one but God, the God who refrains from all forms

1 See René Girard (1978), *Things Hidden Since the Foundation of the World* (trans. Stephen Bann and Michael Meteer) (London: Athlone Books) pp. 284–98.
2 Walter Wink (1992), *Engaging the Powers*, (Minneapolis: Fortress Press) p. 195.

of reprisal and makes his sun to shine upon the "just" and the "unjust" without distinction – this word remains, for him, absolutely valid. It is valid even to death..'[1]

Wink, following Girard, says:

'…the God whom Jesus reveals refrains from all forms of reprisal and demands no victims. God does not endorse holy wars or just wars or religions of violence. Only by being driven out by violence could God signal to humanity that the divine is non-violent and is antithetical to the Kingdom of Violence….The reign of God means the complete and definitive elimination of every form of violence between individuals and nations. This is a realm and a possibility of which those imprisoned by their own espousal of violence cannot even conceive.'[2]

Jesus as Victim

It is helpful to think of Jesus as the one who breaks out of the cycle of human oppression and revenge and shows humanity another way to live (eg Matthew 18.21–22; Luke 6. 27–28), but this way of understanding Jesus' life and teaching is complicated by the way that the Church often speaks of Jesus as victim, for example as 'priest and victim' in the hymn 'Alleluia, sing to Jesus'.[3] The problem arises when Jesus is perceived *only* as victim without reference to the reconciling work done by God in His Son, the reconciling work which offers human beings a way of getting rid of the categories of victims and victimisers for ever. Theology has given us Jesus as the victim of the ritual sacrifice, sent to appease God's anger against human sin by an act of blood and violence which is once and for all. John's gospel sets the Crucifixion in the context of the slaughter of the Passover lambs to make that connection (John 19.31).

How can we make sense of Jesus as resistant to, subversive of, and triumphant over, the powers of evil when he is also presented in art and devotional writing as the helpless Lamb? Girard suggests that we need new pictures to stop us missing out on the totality of Jesus' self-offering in a way which connects his teaching during his ministry, and his death and resurrection more closely. So he argues for a non-sacrificial reading of the Gospels to bring new insight into what Jesus did.[4] Wink argues for a God who turns human violence perpetuated by evil Powers into solidarity with those suffering from it.

Another way of reading of the Gospels shows the differing players in Jerusalem acting according to whether they think Jesus is Victimiser or Victimised. The Jewish authorities and Roman authorities are worried about

---

1 René Girard, op.cit., p. 206.
2 Walter Wink, op.cit., p. 149.
3 For other examples, see Brian Castle, op. cit., pp. 48–9
4 See *Things Hidden from the Foundation of the World* p. 213.

the advent of an avenging Messiah who will overthrow the Roman occupation on the one hand and sweep away religious corruption (as he has already
done in the Temple) on the other. The cheering crowds believe in the cycle
of revenge and think Jesus is going to throw down the mighty and rise up
in messianic glory, a warrior lord like King David. The disciples, however,
are in the presence of someone who says he is going to die, who deliberately
puts himself at risk, and walks straight into the hands of those who are out
to get him. He refuses to fight when his disciples defend him and rejects
violence. Pilate is confused when he treats Jesus as a potential victimiser
who is accused of religious sedition. Jesus talks about power and kingship
all right, but not in a way that makes sense to Pilate's problems with unrests,
zealots and small rebellions.

The outcome of this is that Jesus ends up as the condemned criminal,
giving up his human dignity, his will and his divine power to be put to death
at the hands of the powerful. We tend to focus on his status as the victimised without looking at the attempt by the authorities to present him as the
potential victimiser, to make out that his teaching, healings and ministry
were acts of oppression and threat to the established order. So we have to
say not only that Jesus takes his place among the victimised but that he also
rejects and refuses the status of victimiser that his accusers would place upon
him in condemning him. Here is the final irony of the crown of thorns and
the suggestions that he should use his power to save himself. Yet, though
Jesus died refusing the status of victimiser, Christians have still used his
death as an excuse to victimise others, not recognising that such behaviour
makes it impossible for others to see who Jesus really is.

Cross and Resurrection
The events of Jesus' Passion bring into the experience of God the degrad-
ation of humanity that torture and assault brings to human beings. No one
who has seen Mel Gibson's *The Passion of the Christ* can be left in any doubt
of the brutality of Jesus' experiences on the day of his death. But the resurrection in *this* context is often overlooked, leaving the implication that the
victimhood of Christ is a confirmation of the triumph of evil in this world
– when an innocent person suffers and dies. The resurrection promises that
God's intention is for evil to be overcome and because we know the risen
Jesus, we know that it is true.

Does Jesus 'choose' to be the sacrifice and thereby take his place within
the ultimate outcast community, the community of victimised? If so, Jesus
is at the heart of the victimised community. But portraying Jesus as ultimate Victim without the reconciling work coming from it carries complex
political and unhelpful motifs, including those which led to the persecution
of Jews in retribution for killing Jesus. The early church was an often persecuted community and a theology of persecution and martyrdom is deeply
ingrained in some religions. We can see the fruits of some of this thinking

taken to its extremes in events in our world today. We have to ask where the development of theology has served human ends rather than illuminating the truth about God. We have to decide: was Jesus *ever* a victim?

It matters how we think of and see Christ on the cross because it affects what we offer in Christian witness. Another aspect to this is the issue of power and powerlessness. Reconciliation depends on movement by those who have the power, but reconciliation itself ultimately depends on the victimised one whose desire must be to emerge from the state of being unreconciled with the victimisers. Reconciliation cannot come from the violent or the oppressors. This raises another question about the crucified Jesus and the different theological models of the atonement which exist must be interrogated continuously. The Orthodox see Christ as reigning from the Cross not as the powerless 'victim'. In times past it was even thought wrong to present or imagine Christ, as all powerful God, being victimised. In the Anglo-Saxon poem *The Dream of the Rood*, the poet gets round this problem by having the cross describe the agony of the nails, while Christ himself is a young hero who strides to his cross and embraces it. The crucifixion event unfolds under his command. Milbank talks about the Sovereign Victim, a challenging and paradoxical idea which may help us re-imagine the Christ we share.[1]

---

1 John Milbank (2003), *Being Reconciled: Ontology and Pardon*, (London: Routledge).

Punishment and Liberation

'I was...in prison and you did not visit me.' (Matthew 25.43)

In *A Long Walk to Freedom*, Nelson Mandela reflected that no one understands a country until they have seen inside its prisons.[1] He was able to speak with authority, having been imprisoned for 27 years for supporting the anti-apartheid cause. His experience did not cause him to be consumed with bitterness, but his liberation from prison brought words which amazed everyone. Desmond Tutu writes:

> 'Nelson Mandela did not emerge from prison spewing words of hatred and avenge. He amazed us all by his heroic embodiment of reconciliation and forgiveness. No one could have accused him of speaking glibly and facilely about forgiveness and reconciliation.'[2]

Nelson Mandela also went on to say that the test of a country is how it treats its lowest citizens. How we should treat those with no power and status around us is something which Jesus teaches us by word and deed. Yet if there is a clearly identified community of the Unreconciled, the prison population is surely an obvious example.

In an imperfect world, we have to recognise that some people hurt others and commit crimes. When they do, we have a justice system that deprives people of their liberty and locks them away from the people they have hurt and the people that they might further hurt. Consequently we have to recognise and accept that we live in a punitive society.

To achieve a sentence which properly fits the crime is the measure of 'justice'. Typically, in the media, people who have been affected by terrible crime are asked for their reaction to sentencing and whether justice has been done. Often the prevailing feeling is that no sentence or punishment is enough to 'pay for' a human life.

For example, Adele Eastman, the fiancée of Thomas ap Rhys Pryce who was murdered in January 2006, produced a moving statement of how his death had affected her and her family, saying that she felt as if her heart had been taken out of her body and torn into small pieces.[3] The papers also reported the fact that his teenage murderers showed no apparent remorse and embraced each other in the dock before being taken away. In making such a statement, Ms Eastman identified herself as one of the Unreconciled,

---

1 Nelson Mandela (1995), *A Long Walk to Freedom*, (New York: Back Bay Books).

2 Desmond Tutu (1999), *No Future Without Forgiveness*, (London: Rider), p. 39.

3 The statement was reported in full at http://www.telegraph.co.uk/news/uknews/1535472/ Heart-torn-into-pieces.html.

NELSON MANDELA

unable to reach any kind of peace with the perpetrators and, while rejecting hatred and bitterness, she asked many questions about how the murderers could have come to a place where a man could be killed for an Oyster card and a mobile phone.[1]

Adele Eastman was a particularly articulate and eloquent person who was able to get across her love and loss in a way that deeply affected many people, but this reminds us that there are many who do not have the chance to make such a statement or who would be incapable of doing so and their pain and their questions are not acknowledged or reconciled.

The criminal justice system as we have it in the UK therefore creates two kinds of Unreconciled, the prisoners and the victimised, who thereafter have no means of reconciliation available to them if the prisoner is locked away from the victimised ones and their families. Criminologists differ on whether this system is effective, particularly with respect to the American system of locking more and more people up and creating a culture of 'corrections' that affects many people, whereas some abolitionists think that prisons are not ever the answer.[2] Yet many of the victimised complain that prisoners are released too soon or that sentences are not long enough to 'pay for' the crime. Reconciliation work means looking seriously at issues involved in this. Does locking up people help victimised people psychologically? Are there issues of both security and vindictiveness? Does depriving people of liberty *really* ease pain when so many families make the point that no sentence can give them their murdered family member back again?

It is noticeable that many of the matters in our society which divide people into groups of Unreconciled have the law in the background, but using law to enforce peace or stability without addressing underlying issues is extremely difficult and unsatisfactory as many troubled areas show all too clearly. Enforcement of law reinforces the status of the Unreconciled, making it impossible for new and creative things to happen within a climate of tension and suspicion. As Christians, we need to ask: what has to happen to allow reconciliation to take place and keep the force of law out of the picture. Do we really know how to live continuously as reconciled people?

Mission contrasts how Christians do things with how our dominant culture finds it has to do things. Our culture often reads issues in terms of doves and hawks (like solicitors trying to get couples to mediate but then turning adversarial); law and anarchy; and truth and falsehood (and keeping secrets).For Christians the issues are what Jesus tells us about doves and serpents, law and gospel and speaking the truth in love. Clearly then, what

---

1 Following his murder, his parents, fiancée and work colleagues set up the Tom ap Rhys Pryce Memorial Trust to provide educational or vocational training to underprivileged people and to tackle the root causes of street crime.

2 See for example: Jock Young., 'Charles Young and the American Prison Experiment: the dilemmas of a libertarian' online at http://www.malcolmread.co.uk/JockYoung/murray. htm and Alan Elsner, (2008) *The Gates of Injustice*, (New Jersey: Pearson Education Limited).

society expects to see in terms of criminal justice and peace-keeping, and what Christians expect to see in terms of Kingdom values will be different, and this can lead to both frustration and misunderstanding.

The Hebrew Scriptures offer a number of pictures of an angry, jealous God who thinks nothing of wiping out human beings who displease him. In Genesis chapters 6–8, evil humanity is wiped out by the Flood so that human beings can have a new start. Sodom and Gomorrah are laid waste (Genesis chapters 18–19) and the enemies of Israel are part of a mass extermination perpetrated by God's avenging angel. For example:

> **'That night the angel of the LORD went out and put to death a hundred and eighty-five thousand men in the Assyrian camp. When the people got up the next morning—there were all the dead bodies! So Sennacherib king of Assyria broke camp and withdrew. He returned to Nineveh and stayed there.'**
>
> 2 Kings 19.35–36

In these stories those Unreconciled people who are not at one with God's will are simply destroyed. These events become exemplars of God's purpose and serve to drive home the original message in the expulsion from the Garden of Eden. These dark and terrifying stories of God's power and might are not just illustrations of despotic savagery, but they also serve to heighten the sense of Israel's struggle for liberation, which is tied to the idea of being ethically holy, a light to the nations. Demonstrations of God's punishing power are not ends in themselves, but an historical analysis of the impossibility of prospering in the Unreconciled state. The angel of death sweeping over the face of the earth, makes concrete for the Unreconciled what is already present in their psyche, so to be passed over, to emerge safe, vindicated and whole, as the people of Israel do, becomes a powerful image of rebirth as the Israelites are delivered to safety. Christians often do not like to dwell on the harsh punitive pages of Scripture, because we often don't know what to make of them, but this is a pity as we may miss altogether knowing how the power of God's reconciling will is understood to work itself out in the history of a holy people, trying to make sense of living in violent and unpredictable times.

Punishment

Christopher Marshall writes that:

> '*All* prisons – from the hell holes of Somalia to the enlightened institutions of Scandanavian countries – are warehouses of pain, places where hurt and hurting people are made to suffer further hurt through the forced deprivation of freedom, the loss of autonomy and dignity, and prolonged isolation from the people who care for them most. It is precisely *because* imprisonment hurts that we use it as a punishment in the first place.

Punishment is, by definition, pain delivery, and locking people up is our favoured form of administering punitive pain today.'[1]

The important theological question is: what is the *purpose* of punishment? Many Christians have no real understanding of this important question. How do we think about punishment and the punitive side that is in all of us? There is a part of human nature that wants to make people suffer when we are wronged and before we can attempt reconciliation we need to acknowledge this.

Richard

I went out with a girl called Bethany. I really loved that girl, man. Then she dumped me and went off with some idiot called Reece. First I sat in my room and cried and then I got angry, really angry. I punched my bedroom wall until my hand bled. Then I wanted bad things to happen to them. I thought about it a lot. Maybe she'd get run over. Maybe he'd fall under a train. I started to imagine all sorts of crazy things. I couldn't do anything else except think about it. I wanted to punish them for being together. I wanted them to die. But in the end they were happy and I wasn't. It wasn't a good place to be, man. Don't go there.

Is punishment then a manifestation of the state of being Unreconciled in ourselves? And is resolution something which can only come after punishment or instead of it?

One of our tasks is to think about the language that is in popular use about prisoners, especially the inflammatory language used in the press

1 Christopher D. Marshall, 'Prison, Prisoners and the Bible' a paper delivered to 'Breaking Down the Walls' Conference, Tukua Nga Here Kia Marama Ai Matamata, 14–16 June, 2002, p. 6, online at http://www.restorativejustice.org/10fulltext/marshall-christopher.-prison-prisoners-and-the-bible/view.

about sex offenders. The fact that sex offenders are, like us, also created in the image of God is problematic, since such people are often demonized, dehumanized and described as 'beasts' or 'monsters' in the popular press.[1] The churches need to tackle such a theological task but it is difficult – saying or writing things in defence of sex offenders can create the perception that there is something to criticise in those who have been hurt or killed by such offenders and this can create an enormous emotional backlash in the popular mind. How then is it possible to speak of sex offenders and how they might be reconciled to their communities? This question is particularly acute with the rolling out of 'Sarah's Law' in England and Wales by 2011. There are already debates about whether making the whereabouts of convicted sex offenders known will lead to driving them underground or lead to vigilantism by the public.[2] In either case, released sex offenders would be placed permanently in an Unreconciled community of their own. Further, it has also been suggested that if such people find themselves cut off from opportunities to work and live normally, they may become more likely to re-offend.

Alongside this problem is another: the pastoral support of prisoners' families. While released prisoners have problems being released into the community, the families of prisoners may also find themselves victimised so that people find themselves vilified and persecuted. Families of terrorists, sex offenders and murderers somehow have to go on living in their communities, shopping, going to school, facing their neighbours. Sometimes the shame and stigma that is attached to the crime makes the family's life a misery for years. Sometimes people need help to bear the fact that someone they love has committed a terrible and incomprehensible crime.

So who *is* a criminal? A criminal is one who has crossed a particular kind of threshold, or legal or moral line. A burglar crosses the threshold of a person's home, or private space, invades that space and damages it. Even if a burglar takes nothing, people report a sense of violation from the very fact that someone has entered their home uninvited. Violent crime crosses the line of a person's body space, invading that body and wounding it, perhaps permanently. Murderers cross the line between a person's life and their death, and, most hated of all, sex offenders may cross the line between the protection of the vulnerable and exploiting and abusing them. As human beings, we keep inside these lines when we are law abiding, but our understanding of good and right behaviour is *more* than this – it has to do with the recognition of the spaces in which human beings need to live and our need to honour and protect them. Law abiding behaviour is not an absence of criminality, but something more; recognition that our lives involve protecting people who need such protection, our bodies are temples

---

1 See Brian Castle, op.cit, pp. 83–4.
2 See BBC News UK, 1st August 2010 'Police doubt "Sarah's Law" will cause vigilante attacks' online at http://www.bbc.co.uk/news/uk-10827669.

of a divine spirit and that the abuse of power utterly violates such community. Therefore most perpetrators are effectively outcasts, marginalised by
their crimes and excluding themselves from society by their behaviour. In a
punitive society, we add to that marginalisation by imprisonment, effectively
marking the prisoner as one who is other, not us, rejected and sent away
by the community. The media often add to this by the use of demonising
language for sensational crimes, which then colours the public view and
discourse about them. Many people are affected by the view of prison we
get from American movies. But that culture does not represent the culture
of real prisons.

So do we continue to think of prisoners as real people with an impact
on the world? A current question is whether prisoners' human rights come
before other considerations and if their human rights are violated, how does
that relate to the attitude of the punitive society? For example, one major
question following a European ruling in 2005 is whether some prisoners
should continue to have the right to vote. Are they still within the democracy
or have they put themselves beyond the right to participate in (law-abiding)
society?[1]

Tom Wallace (Taxpayers Alliance)

**It would be disgusting to let tens of thousands of criminals have an equal vote
as the law abiding majority. These convicts never gave a second thought to the
rights of others when they committed their crimes so their right to vote should
be forfeited.[2]**

. . . .

In general, prisoners are excluded from all freedoms, so perhaps
extending to them any part of the democratic system is a gesture towards
a reconciling process.

Addiction and crime

We tend to assume that a criminal is someone who has made a choice not
to follow society's laws and conventions and indeed has made a choice
about the costs and benefits of committing crime,[3] but this is to ignore the
fact that many prisoners commit crime because they are not in their 'right
minds'. They are, to use a biblical phrase, possessed by demons. For many,
that demon is heroin addiction. For a £100 a day habit a person may need to
steal £400–£500 worth of goods a day. This generates an enormous amount
of crime.

---

1 See http://www.bbc.co.uk/news/uk-11671164

2 Robert Winnett and Tom Whitehead (09/04/2009) 'Prisoners get right to vote after 140
years following European ruling' online at http://www.telegraph.co.uk/news/uknews/law-
and-order/5126647/Prisoners-to-get-right-to-vote-after-140-years-following-European-
ruling.html

3 Sociologists and criminologists talk about 'rational choice theory'.

Rob English (former heroin addict)

I was addicted to heroin for 23 years, from the age of 15 to 38. I lived on the street, squatted and went in and out of prisons. It wasn't a life choice at 15. I was self-medicating at home because I was brought up around alcohol and Valium, which my father used. He was aggressive. I tried to run away three times – first at 12, then 13, and then finally at 15. I ended up on the streets in London, where I met a lot of other distressed young people who were self-medicating.I spent quite a lot of time in prison – I think I went in a total of nine or 10 times – because you will do anything to feed your habit. It controls you and you are its servant. You will either resort to crime or to drug dealing because those are the only ways to fund your habit.My addiction cost £200 a day and it wasn't numbing me any more, my tolerance was so high. I believed I was going to die that way.Every time we left prison with our medication, we'd be selling it by the time we got to the prison gates.I tried to give up in rehab when I was 34 but I got thrown out after 28 days for being disruptive. I remember being in tears as I walked out of the gates and I was already back on heroin by the time my train pulled into King's Cross.When I finally gave up at 38, it took me 12 months to stabilise myself on methadone. I have seen what methadone addiction can do.[1]

Addicted people who commit crimes often become wedded to an Unreconciled community, from which, as seen above, it can be incredibly difficult to break out.

Similarly some prisoners suffer from mental illnesses which manifest themselves in crime. Our society enables us to punish the crimes but we have fewer resources to treat the illness. Yet Jesus asks us find and help those cast out and suffering the stigmatism, fear and misery of mental illness. 'Care in the community' suggests that all of us should play a part in caring for those less fortunate than ourselves, but often we completely fail to look after those who cannot take care of themselves easily. People who should be cared for and looked after may end up neglected and overlooked. For example, it was reported on 3 August 2010 that a woman who looked after her disabled daughter died suddenly at her home and the daughter, unable to care for herself or summon help, simply starved to death. Similarly, people with mental illness who need care and concern can be neglected and ignored until they commit crimes which we then demand to see punished. The failure of our duty should make us complicit in the crime, but we do not care to consider that aspect, blaming the person who has been failed by us. As Christians we should have a commitment to prophetic witness about the radical reconciliation which needs to take place to establish peace – a society as free as possible from crime because we all accept our responsibilities for the Unreconciled groups like those with addictions and those with mental illness, properly.

---

1 From Jeremy Laurence, 'Heroin: the solution?' *The Independent*, 2nd June 2006 online at http://www.independent.co.uk/news/uk/crime/heroin-the-solution-480734.html

We can take a model for this in the story of the Gerasene demoniac (Mark 5.1–20). The man is found raving in his mental affliction, his humanity ruined. He is outcast, has been repeatedly chained up, driven to a distant place away from human society. He is an archetypal member of an Unreconciled society of the criminally insane from whom all reasonable people would keep away. Jesus however, comes to the man and ignores his outward appearance and behaviour. In talking to the man, he searches for the image of God in him, his essential self which is presented to us as a dialogue between Jesus and the demons who control the man's wretched life. When the man is delivered, he is restored to the man he was supposed to be under God 'clothed and in his right mind'. He is capable of re-entering society and talking about his transformation. All that was ever possible before was containment of his affliction, but Jesus makes it clear that it is imperative to go beyond this, to make not only restoration, but something *new*, a person with a new vision and clear sighted understanding of life in God's world. The man is effectively reborn. But what is most interesting in the story is the reaction of the people in the country of the Gerasenes. *They are frightened to death and want Jesus to go away.* We would rather chain people up than face the prospect of their restoration.

Imprisonment

The truth is simply that the needs of our society to imprison perpetrators sets up an impenetrable barrier to a reconciled, Kingdom society. Imprisonment is the sign of a divided society far from God's intention, by keeping among us a community of permanently Unreconciled people. Prisoners do not represent a cross section of society; the majority are young, male, addicted and poor. Most prisoners carry the stamp of disadvantage and have been failed by our society.

SOME PRISON STATISTICS

Many prisoners have experienced a lifetime of social exclusion. Compared with the general population, prisoners are **thirteen** times as likely to have been in care as a child, **thirteen** times as likely to be unemployed, **ten** times as likely to have been a regular truant, **two and a half times** as likely to have had a family member convicted of a criminal offence, **six** times as likely to have been a young father, and **fifteen** times as likely to be HIV positive.

Many prisoners' basic skills are very poor. **80 per cent** have the writing skills, **65 per cent** the numeracy skills and **50 per cent** the reading skills at or below the level of an 11-year-old child. **60 to 70 per cent** of prisoners were using drugs before imprisonment. Over **70 per cent** suffer from at least two mental disorders. And **20 per cent** of male and **37 per cent** of female sentenced prisoners have attempted suicide in the past. The position is often even worse for 18–20-year-olds, whose

basic skills, unemployment rate and school exclusion background are all over **a third** worse than those of older prisoners.

Despite high levels of need, many prisoners have effectively been excluded from access to services in the past. It is estimated that around **half** of prisoners had no GP before they came into custody; prisoners are over **twenty** times more likely than the general population to have been excluded from school; and one prison drugs project found that although **70 per cent** of those entering the prison had a drug misuse problem, **80 per cent** of these had never had any contact with drug treatment services.

There is a considerable risk that a prison sentence might actually make the factors associated with reoffending worse. For example, **a third** lose their house while in prison, **two-thirds** lose their job, **over a fifth** face increased financial problems and **over two-fifths** lose contact with their family. There are also real dangers of mental and physical health deteriorating further, of life and thinking skills being eroded, and of prisoners being introduced to drugs. By aggravating the factors associated with re-offending, prison sentences can prove counter-productive as a contribution to crime reduction and public safety.[1]

These statistics show that we lock up the poorest people from the poorest areas. A high proportion of such people have never been schooled and never worked. They become dependent upon drugs, especially heroin, and spiral downwards out of control. Women in prison are often themselves victims of abuse in the first place.

Around 85,000 of the most excluded people in Britain are left in prison at any one time.[2] They are there because of a need to increase public safety and in the name of justice. But God speaks to us of the justice they too deserve and there is no strategy which so far has made any real headway in raising them up and giving it to them. God's vision is not that the tears of the victimised should be dried, but that the perpetrators should never have life stories leading them to cause that pain in the first place. Reconciliation for these Unreconciled needs to begin with telling this truth and addressing it. If there has to be punishment in our punitive society it has to be useful punishment which offers people a way out of their Unreconciled state, otherwise there is merely immorality and waste in the huge amounts of money spent on putting and keeping people in prison (around £37,500 pa each in 2002). Christian understanding of these issues can be often muddled and incoherent. We don't know why we imprison other human beings, but equally we don't know if we shouldn't and what else we could do. But a vision of a Kingdom community which lives according to God's

1 *Reducing Re-offending by ex-prisoners*, summary of Social Exclusion Unit report, 2002, pp. 2–3.
2 Weekly population figures are available at www.hmprisonservice.gov.uk.

will and God's intention for human beings is impossible if there are people in prison who should not be there. For the majority of us then, prisons as institutions are unintelligible, incomprehensible. Unless we have ever been inside one or visited someone there, they remain for us unknown and unimaginable places.[1]

However, at the same time we should realize that we should be concerned and involved with what goes on inside the prison system because the treatment of prisoners is the test of a compassionate society. It requires heart searching by those who are charged with punishment; an attempt to rehabilitate those who commit crimes, the putting in place of curative and regenerating processes and the recognition that there is treasure in every heart. Where we engage in reconciling work of this kind, reaching out to those Unreconciled within the justice system then we can offer living virtues to our society. This means we can find out how to 'put up' with prisons by initiating and sustaining the seeds of reconciliation. If we want to examine the mission imperative to reconcile, then a good place to start is in those areas where the processes of our society inevitably do harm. We can see this harm at work in the following story:

A GIRL...

...was convicted of having drugs at school. She was sentenced and detained and then appealed. While this was happening she left school and got a job. She found a boyfriend and become pregnant. She was

sent to prison. When this happened her boss wrote to say she had lost her job. Two weeks later, her boyfriend said that he wasn't coping and would have to give up their house. He left her. She went into premature labour and her baby was born in prison.

· ·

This is a model of the kind of harm that prisons do. Families disintegrate, jobs are lost.

It is not a matter of treatment or rehabilitation being available in prison which is designed to put people back on track, when the structure for their meaningful life crumbles outside. The fact of prison does harm.

In addition, the presence of pain and suffering within prisons indicts our own society. If we send people to prison, we should surely be responsible for finding ways to do good within the Unreconciled community of the imprisoned and to bring about forms of reconciliation. In general, we know that reconciling work flourishes when it is present in individual relationships, such as between prisoners and staff, but overcrowding and lack of resources is a threat to such relationships. Prison staff do most of the important reconciling work, but they are often forgotten and need support. Prison dehumanises people and also institutionalises them, so prison staff have the additional task of trying to prepare prisoners to be reconciled to life outside prison when they are released.[1] The intention is to equip them on release no longer to be alienated members of society, but capable of productive contribution. The most significant factor in this is engagement between prison staff and prisoners in guiding prisoners through work/education programmes to address offending behaviour and 'throughcare'.

This reconciling work needs to be engaged with support in the community and to find ways of re-presenting prisoners as restored and forgiven. Such rehabilitation makes no sense without housing, freedom from addiction, and proper employment, but the throughcare designed to achieve this is often ineffective or lacking. This is evident from the fact that a large number of prisoners reoffend within two years of release:

─ PRISON SENTENCES... ─────────────────────────

... are not succeeding in turning the majority of offenders away from crime. Of those prisoners released in 1997, **58 per cent** were convicted of another crime within two years. **36 per cent** were back inside on another prison sentence. The system struggles particularly to reform younger offenders. 18–20-year-old male prisoners were reconvicted at a rate of **72 per cent** over the same period; **47 per cent** received another prison sentence.[2]

· ·

---

1 In the film *The Shawshank Redemption*, a prisoner risks further punishment by broadcasting classical music to the inmates, who are transformed for a short space, by the power of the music, a symbol of the world that is denied them.

2 *Op. cit.*, p. 1.

The number of small time offenders who reoffend is very high despite all the programmes: '…more than two thirds of ex-offenders re-offend and are returned to prison within 2 years. This figure is a few percentage points higher for those ex-offenders aged 18–21.'[1] Reconciliation work for those who have offended requires not only finding the treasure in their hearts but providing a future environment in which it can grow.

Beyond the limits of contempt: sex offenders

The issue of the demonization of sex offenders is just as acute within prison itself. Wherever they are held prisons have to go to lengths to give them special consideration, especially in the provision of food and exercise. This is because within prison, sex offenders form a particular group of Unreconciled. There are unreconciled issues between sex offenders and every other prisoner because 'ordinary' prisoners themselves feel contempt and hatred for sex offenders. This reflects opinion in society, our own natures, and reporting by the media. The presence of sex offenders is a significant factor in running jails and something which cannot be easily reconciled. Sex offenders remain therefore the lowest of the low and this raises huge issues for staff, society and the prisoners themselves. What is the Christian response to people who are 'beyond the pale' and what kind of reconciling work can offer them back to society?[2] Even Christians will sometimes baulk at the idea of standing up for an Ian Brady or an Ian Huntley, but who are such people before God and how can God's longing for them be translated into restitution and recovery?

The TV drama *Longford* looked at the relationship between Frank Pakenham, Lord Longford and Myra Hindley and at his Christian conviction that even the most demonized and hated person is worthy of redemption and of a second chance. The drama looked at the difficulties of such an attempt at reconciliation. Lord Longford was himself vilified for trying to befriend Hindley and for campaigning for her release and the film asked whether she genuinely wanted to reform or was merely playing a part, using him and stringing him along, because as a Christian he was naïve or blinkered to her evil nature. Yet at the end of the film, Hindley is portrayed making a genuine move towards Longford without agenda and Longford says that he regrets nothing because just knowing her has enriched his life. The film suggests that demonization of people damages all of us and the generosity of spirit which can enable us to find God's image in every person is a powerful reconciling force.[3]

How then can Christians work with models of reconciliation to help

1 Citizens Online and National Centre for Social Research (2008) *Digital Exclusion Profiling of Vulnerable Groups: ex-offenders* (London: HMSO) p. 7.
2 See Church of England Board of Social Responsibility, (1999) *Prisons, a study in vulnerability* (London: Church House Publishing).
3 See Brian Castle, op.cit., pp. 84–5.

offenders become who they were meant to be before God and help society to face them rather than lock them up and forget about them? One problem is that we have no good account of why we have prisons at all. Being inside is something no one really understands. We need to engage those hostile to the Christian understanding that we are all made in the image of God, but too often we shy away from it and become guarded about the big questions.[1]

'Prison hurts because it contradicts our humanity. We are made as free creatures in the image of a freedom-loving God. To take that freedom away from people is to exercise an awesome responsibility because it strikes at the heart of human dignity and identity.'[2]

Prisoners and reconciliation

Clearly the people who work at the coal face in this regard are prison chaplains and volunteers. Yet some prison chaplains are aware how little they are actually able to speak about guilt and about the forgiveness of Christ. Spiritual life is an important area of the life of prisoners and yet there is so little addressing these issues or equipping people to deal with them. Prison staff don't necessarily talk about guilt, repentance or forgiveness. While we might expect prison chaplains to do this routinely it is not always easy to allow these issues to be mentioned. This means that we should try to get better at dealing with the spiritual lives of prisoners at a deep level. To reach such a community of Unreconciled we need to identify what is not helpful and clear a path for people to begin to explore those things which are meaningful to them.

Research has been done to find out what Bible stories are liked best by people in different sections of society. Most people like the Parable of the Good Samaritan or the Prodigal Son. For prisoners it turns out that the story which speaks most to them is the story of Peter trying to walk on the water (Matthew 14.22–33). The man drowning reflects their own story. They don't believe that they too can be raised from the depths – but they wish it were true.

Somehow we need to find the courage to face the fact of people who have raped and murdered and are in prisons and to face the questions they raise which we would rather run away from.

Joe (police officer)

In my heart I really do think that we are involved in reconciliation, but most of the public we serve don't see us like that. For example, we get called out to sort out fights, disputes, silliness at closing time and we get in there trying to calm things down, let people have a say and then encourage them to cool off and leave

---

1 Useful papers from the Church of England on matters of criminal justice helping Christians to think through the issues can be found at http://www.churchofengland.org/our-views/home-and-community-affairs/home-affairs-policy/justice-issues-prisons.aspx.
2 Christopher Marshall, op.cit., p. 6.

it alone. Sometimes a situation that's flared up can be cooled down quite easily and the people involved forget whatever the problem was and go off again best buddies. Our main problem is when there are weapons involved and somebody gets hurt before we've got time to get there. It's tragic. Once the damage is done there's no way back; they're in the system.

A lot of people think we're the bad guys. But we are helpers, we're just not seen that way. We do have to catch villains and put them away so there's peace, but sometimes we lean the other way, giving people a chance to sort their lives out and go in another direction. Some kids....they break your heart. But sometimes you do see it, some sort of reconciliation, when kids who've got sucked in with the wrong crowd, got the drugs, the drink, whatever, manage to break out of it. You get pretty cynical about whether people are ever going to change, but just sometimes – it's fantastic.

Restorative Justice

An important concept in reconciliation work aimed at offenders and those they victimise is Restorative Justice. Its key ideas are important for Christians, since restorative justice appeals to the needs of the victimised. In the court the needs of victimised are sometimes marginalised and even ignored. Restorative justice argues that participation by those victimised by offenders helps both the hurt person and the perpetrator. Restorative justice seeks to help, encourage, and even demand of perpetrators to understand what they have done. It requires people to hear, to learn, to know about damage, the cost and the hurt. So restorative justice involves giving something back. When offenders are faced with the needs of those they have hurt, it encourages them to face up to their responsibilities and start to make reparation. We can see that this concept goes beyond offence and punishment. An habitual offender often becomes locked into a cycle of doing crime and then doing time. Restorative justice seeks to interrupt that cycle by making the victims of crime part of the criminal's mental view, asking them to be responsible.

A PLEA...

Would the heartless person who stole my daughter's bicycle last Friday from ...... please think again and return it? It was a present for her birthday from her granddad and she hasn't stopped crying since it was stolen. You know who you are. Please do the decent thing.

Letter in a local newspaper

This public appeal occasionally works. Fences or others passing on stolen goods have been known to return them or make them available if they become aware of a person's pain, particularly if the victimised person is elderly or a child. There is sometimes honour among thieves.

The Restorative Justice Movement is well developed in New Zealand and there are projects in the UK as well. A project in the North East of England, in the words of one prison officer, suggests that justice is 'putting back'. The Church should be able to help with models of restorative justice, both with those in prison and those in the community. For victims to meet their victimisers and to hear them say that they are sorry really can help them and make a big difference, but this means management of the process and enabling a language of mutuality.[1]

Imprisonment and reconciliation

Only speaking the truth can bring about reconciliation for such groups of the Unreconciled as we send to our prisons. The silences of society and church about the reality of prison makes reconciliation difficult. We all tend to be quiet about prisons. Yet prison reform has in the past been motivated by Christian faith, following the example and command of Jesus. As Christians, therefore, we should want to change the conditions of prisoners.

---

1 Work has been done by Andrew Coyle, Professor of Prison Studies at KCL at the International Centre for Prison Studies. See http://www.kcl.ac.uk/schools/law/research/icps. Other places for this include the Prison Fellowship which has a Restorative Justice programme and the Sycamore Tree Programme http://www.prisonfellowship.org.uk/sycamore-tree.html. Also see Peter Sedgwick (ed. 2004) *Re-thinking Sentencing* (London: Church House Publishing).

This truth needs to be offered in two ways. We need to tell the truth about the terrible damage caused by overcrowding in prisons and we need to find a way to give an account of what a 'good' prison might be. Overcrowding means that restorative and liberating programmes have to be put aside for crisis management. People have to be processed, they cannot have their humanity recognised and responded to. Similarly treatment for sex offenders can work, but there is so little facility. The waiting time for the programmes can be longer than the sentences.

The churches as agents of liberation and reconciliation

'Perhaps the greatest evangelistic task facing the churches today is a conversion from the spirit of punishment to the spirit of healing'.[1] In thinking about this task we can put together some areas where the churches can help, particularly where there are known factors which influence reoffending.[2] In particular:

+ The families of prisoners need love, care and support. In many cases they may need help to bear what their family member has done. Providing this help preserves the vision of the Kingdom, the hope of salvation, and has knock on effects for public safety. Pastoral care in the Christian community of prisoners' families is a powerful model of reconciliation for mission.

+ People need homes to go to because people who find themselves homeless tend to reoffend. Raising up the poor and helping people to achieve personal autonomy is both reconciliatory and missiological.

+ People need useful employment. If ex-prisoners can find jobs they are much less likely to reoffend. The churches should pioneer care for ex-prisoners, the 'lost' people. A theological conversation could also consider whether redressing the balance means giving ex-prisoners various sorts of special, preferential treatment. How could the churches help; how can the churches engage effectively with justice issues? These things can all contribute to helping us face the Unreconciled with love and care.

+ Many people in prison are mentally ill. Christians can, through the example of Jesus, speak about the need to provide support for such people and the need to provide healing contexts.

---

1 T. Richard Snyder (2001), *The Protestant Ethic and the Spirit of Punishment* (Grand Rapids, Michigan: Eerdmans) p. 155.

2 In November 2010, Ministry of Justice figures for re-offending showed that 74% of people released from custody in 2000 reconvicted within 9 years. See http://www.justice.gov.uk/compendium-reoffending.htm.

Wounds and Healing

Thomas A Tweed writes that 'Religions are confluences of organic-cultural flows that intensify joy and confront suffering by drawing on human and supra-human forces to make homes and cross boundaries'. [1]

Faith in Christ, within the body of Christ, the Christian community, presses us to seek out Unreconciled people, crossing boundaries to find them, and to make homes where we can dwell together. Our task is to confront suffering where we find it and seek, in Tweed's words, to 'intensify joy' – to bring a *new* thing, through love and healing, out of disorder and damage. To overcome evil and suffering, we must look for means of reconciliation, not just to put sticking plasters on wounds but to create new possibilities and hope, to bring joy.

This need to confront suffering is written into the *missio dei*, God's mission of love to the world, and therefore is also part of the mission task given to human beings. We must work against evils which cause suffering wherever we find them. Some events such as natural disasters and the death of living things are part of the experience of life on this planet. In the BBC TV programme, *The Power of the Planet*, Dr Iain Stewart spoke of the risky relationship human beings have always had with dangerous places. On the fault lines of tectonic plates, prone to earthquakes and volcanic eruptions, rich minerals and fertile soils are found, so that is where we like to live, prosper and grow. So we cannot set ourselves against volcanoes and earthquakes, which give us life as well as take it away. But we can seek to prepare ourselves and others for living among dangers and we can confront the suffering which comes when the earthquake happens. We cross boundaries, make new homes and seek to intensify joy. For example, in July 2010, it was reported that a mother who believed her child had been killed in the Haiti earthquake six months earlier was reunited with her daughter in the UK. The child had been pulled alive from the wreckage of a hospital and flown through the good offices of the charity Facing the World (www.facingtheworld.net) to receive medical care. That same charity made it possible for mother and daughter to be reunited.[2] Marie's words on seeing her daughter Landina bring it home to us: 'When I saw her I was amazed. I couldn't believe she was alive. This is a very happy moment'. As in Jesus' parables of those lost and found, we also commit ourselves to such meetings and healings. We work for the intensification of joy.

---

1 Thomas A. Tweed (2006) *Crossing and Dwelling, a theory of religion* (Cambridge, Mass.: Harvard University Press), p. 54.

2 *Metro* 29 July 2010 'Reunited at last with "dead" daughter, the mother called "Miracle"' p. 1.

Christians are also called to confront the evils we are capable of perpetrating on one another and to find ways to care for, heal, and help those affected by the unavoidable pain of living. None of us are immune to these experiences and in normal life, they enter into our histories and stories, not least how we passed through them and overcame them. We become aware of physical pain, which may mean that we are hurt or ill, or that somebody or something has inflicted pain upon us. With physical pain comes mental pain, the experiences of fear, grief, anxiety, hopelessness, despair. Other kinds of psychological pain can be visited upon us, being lied to, being betrayed, being shunned, bullied, emotionally abused. Both mental and physical pain can be experienced as the result of abuse of power, together with disabling emotions such as grief, shame and guilt. For many people, experiences like this are mercifully brief and full recovery is possible. For others, there is serious physical and psychological damage that can last a lifetime. Such evil may also damage individual human relations, or cause trouble in a community, but it may also be magnified into atrocity and genocide. We are called to confront such suffering wherever we can and release those who suffer into new life and hope.

Kobi (video rental store worker)

There ain't none [reconciliation]. That's why I'm not twiddling my fingers in here. You come in here and take a dream home with you, so you don't think about nothing no more.

. . . .

If we call those people Unreconciled who are physically or mentally hurt, damaged by other people, abused or overpowered, then the reconciling acts needed to restore them must come from human will, determination and intent to understand and overcome these causes of evil. Such reconciliation in mission must put energy into healing and mending those affected by evil deeds and also try to transform the hearts of those who would pursue acts of evil. This is profound mission work because it relates directly to the intention of the *missio dei* and the purposes of God. We don't just want to bind up the wounded, but also to redeem the oppressors whose humanity is also ruined by their own evil. We can understand everything we need to know about how this works by reference to Jesus' teaching and work in the Gospels.

Reconciliation in relation to healing.

Human beings have, over centuries of culture and civilisation, developed techniques to heal people of their illnesses. But despite high tech machinery, complex drugs and skilled procedures, treating people who are suffering through illness requires skill in reconciling the sick person to themselves, and involves more than the skills of doctors and surgeons, but also others such as nurses, physiotherapists, counsellors, hospice workers and patients' families and friends. This reconciliation process may mean helping a person whose identity and self will is eroded by the illness to reconcile themselves to a future picture of themselves as healthy person who will leave hospital and resume active life. The reconciliation process may also require helping a person see beyond a permanent change and disability to a future of different possibilities. It may also mean helping a person accept their death and helping them get the most out of what remains of their living, as well as looking forward to a reconciliation beyond death.

Maria (nurse)

My job involves helping people come to terms with the health problems they have. Reconciliation for them means learning to live with a life just below their expectations. A lot of the people I see aren't content with what they've got; they can't find it in them to count their blessings. So they complain about the lack of perfect health and they come back again and again looking for something I can't give them. It's people who are really genuinely ill or dying who become reconciled to their life. But the moaners and complainers who turn up with a succession of 'aches and pains' they're the ones who will never be reconciled to their lot. They get on my nerves.

. . . .

Philippa (plaster technician)

I look after people who have had accidents, putting limbs in plaster. One of the things I notice about people who have had accidents, is they think first of all that the doctors and nurses are miracle workers – once I've put them in plaster that's it, they're mended, they're fine again. But of course it isn't like that. When they realise that it's going to take a lot of time, maybe physio, they get depressed, even angry, it's like, 'where's the magic solution'. That's when they need to get reconciled to the idea that they really have had an accident and no matter what happened or whose 'fault' it is, they have to get on with the job of getting better, slowly, and dealing with the consequences. When the plaster comes off you can see they're sometimes a different person. They've learned something, patience maybe. But then sometimes they're back again with something else broken the next week. They haven't learned anything

. . . .

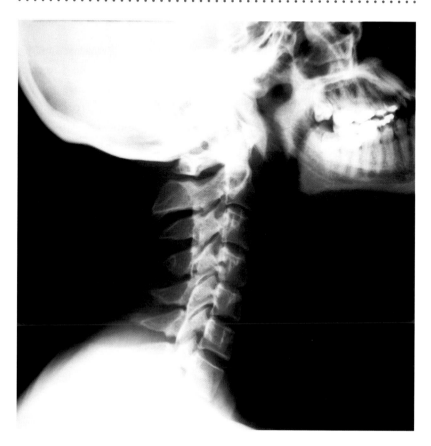

The presence of 'complainers' in our lives tells us that there is a general sense that there is something basically wrong with the world, whether that is a health issue or a sense that society has gone bad, but too often we tune such complainers out. The fact that people also sometimes never seem to learn leads to a feeling that nothing ever really changes. What we see in these two stories is a profoundly theological process because it depends on a sense of our imperfect bodies as measured against an ideal or perfect self, that which is made in the image of God. This ideal personhood exists in God's being and in God's memory and is promised to us as contained in our ultimate destiny beyond the decay of our physical bodies, what David Ford calls 'waiting for the beauty'.[1] The healing of wounds can presuppose an eschatological requirement; the eschaton *is* the moment of final healing/forgiveness.

As Jurgen Moltmann writes:

> 'As Paul says in 1 Cor 15, only with the resurrection of the dead, the murdered and the gassed, only with the healing of those in despair who bear lifelong wounds, only with the abolition of all rule and authority, only with the annihilation of death will the Son hand over the kingdom to the Father. Then God will turn his sorrow into eternal joy.'[2]

Jesus as healer

John V. Taylor reminds us that Jesus' healing miracles are not just a matter of waving a magic wand at people and finding that all illness and deformity has disappeared. Rather, healing is closely bound up with issues of faith, trust and human will and is the outcome of a turning away from inward hopelessness, and being mired in the Unreconciled condition. This is true for both those who would be healed and the disciples who would do the healing. In talking about the crippled man at the pool of Bethesda, John V Taylor says that Jesus first had to reach into the heart of the man's problem and challenge him about it:

> '*When Jesus saw him lying there and was aware that he had been ill a long time, he asked him "Do you want to recover?"* That was a devastatingly perceptive question. For like so many people in deep depression the man believes he is the victim of other people's indifference. *"Sir," he replied, "I have no one to put me in the pool when the water is disturbed, but while I am moving, someone else is in the pool before me..." Jesus answered, "Rise to your feet, take up your pallet bed and walk".* By commanding the impossible – "Stand up" – Jesus simply

---

1 David Ford (1997), *The Shape of Living*, (London: Fount paperbacks) pp. 101–4.
2 Jurgen Moltmann (1974), *The Crucified God*, (London: SCM) pp. 287–8.

defied the man's inveterate, sulky dependence and released in him a new responsibility for his own life. *The man recovered instantly, took up his pallet and began to walk.*'[1]

Scars

Edward Shillito's poem *Jesus of the Scars* reminds us that Jesus is the Wounded Healer who makes it possible for us too to receive healing: 'But to our wounds only God's wounds can speak/And not a god has wounds but thou alone'.[2]

Charlotte (former pole-vaulter)[3]

... battles with the surgery that has left the 34-year-old with scars both on the outside and within.

Her bright pink walking cane hints at the sassy fashion retail manager she used to be but the rest of Charlotte's confidence is on the shelf.

At home the mirrors are all set too high so she doesn't have to face herself, and despite living less than a mile from the beach, Charlotte avoids taking daughter Lana, as that would mean having to strip off.

· ·

In the popular Channel 4 programme How to Look Good Naked, the fashion expert Gok Wan features a person in each episode who has no confidence in her body and often because her body is scarred or damaged.[4] In an episode in July 2010, Charlotte, whose esteem and body confidence had been lost because of the presence of scars was encouraged to see the scars as part of her story, to allow the scars to be touched and to accept her body. The programme uses clothes to help women feel more confident, to love themselves and to develop a positive body image. Gok Wan's own role is to provide positive comments about 'my girl', to show encouragement, support and affection, to receive tears and fears without criticism and to go through the person's journey with them, as anxiety and self-doubt is (usually) replaced by gratitude and joy. However the final part of the programme is to enable the person to shed all the new clothes and accessories and accept their body by being photographed 'naked'. In interviews with Gok Wan about his relationship with each of 'his' girls, he talks about his own experiences of being one of the Unreconciled as a young person which now enables him to empathise with his subjects: he was overweight, is mixed-race and gay.[5]

---

1 John V Taylor, (1998) *The Uncancelled Mandate* (London: Church House Publishing) pp. 12–13.

2 Quoted in John Stott, (1986) *The Cross of Christ* (Nottingham: Inter-Varsity Press) p. 389.

3 Originally quoted at http://www.channel4.com/4beauty/on-tv/how-to-look-good-naked/series-7/how-to-look-good-naked-charlotte.

4 We use this example, because of the interest this programme has generated with groups of young people with whom we have been working.

5 See Rachel Cooke 'In Gok we Trust' in *The Observer* 4 November 2007 online at http://www.guardian.co.uk/lifeandstyle/2007/nov/04/fashion.features10.

How to Look Good Naked deals with those who have low confidence and low self-esteem. Such wounds are addressed by attention from Gok, gifts of clothes, and pampering, very much in tune with a consumerist and individualised world. The new thing which is brought to birth is wrought from hair and make-up artists and Gok's eye for fashion. Yet in the end, what is underneath has to be addressed, the scars acknowledged, the disfigurement transformed from something that exiles and alienates into something which represents story and survival and of which those bearing them should not be ashamed.

Deformity

But there are also those whose damage cannot be redeemed in this way and who need our help on quite another level. In another Channel 4 television programme, My New Face, on November 15th 2006, two surgeons Norman Waterhouse and Matthew Kelly, also from the Facing the World charity mentioned above, who are skilled in facial and cranial surgery, talked about the work they do with children and young people in developing countries who suffer from facial deformity.[1] The programme followed the stories of two such children in particular, Arianto, who suffers from neurofibromatosis affecting one side of his face and Ney, whose facial disfigurement had caused him to be stoned by others in his village. Both these children were condemned through no fault of their own to live Unreconciled lives, unaccepted and unintegrated into their communities.

One moving scene in the programme featured Arianto looking in a mirror so that the 'good' half of his face was reflected, giving him a whole, symmetrical face of the way he 'should have been' without the disease. That wholeness and symmetry could not be achieved by the surgeons, but his operations were intended to use as much medical skill and technology as possible to help him move towards that ideal of symmetrical features that everyone with facial features in the right place takes for granted. The task was to line up his features so that people would be able to 'see' Arianto as a person properly.[2] At each stage Arianto had to be reconciled to his face and each change promised him more acceptance in his own community and the chance of a better life. Arianto's changes were also set in the context of his profound faith in God, which enabled him to be reconciled to the presence of his disease, and to have hope that his life could be improved. With Ney, the surgery was so much more than cosmetic – a means of reconciling him to his community so that he could live in peace without being outcast, and the programme brought this home by filming the reunion with his family,

---

1 www.channel4.com/health/microsites/M/my_new_face/index.html.

2 Conversely, when the Weta workshop were working on the appearance of Wormtongue in The Lord of the Rings, they deliberately gave him different coloured eyes, shaved off his eyebrows and made his face assymetrical in order to suggest evil, distortion and untrustworthiness.

and showing images of him playing in the street with other children. This also raises another question about why it takes such surgery to enable him to be reconciled with his community. Part of the mission task in these matters is to help people be reconciled with the idea of the disabled and different among them, because all of us are still 'waiting for the beauty'. Both How to Look Good Naked and My New Face contrast sharply with the trend for purely cosmetic surgery, helping people find acceptance in their less than perfect bodies.

Wounds

What is a wound? A wound is damage to the wholeness of the body, a brokenness which typically causes pain. A natural human response to a wounded being is shock, and horror and perhaps fear, but also compassion and a desire to make it right. Everyone knows the nuisance of rubber necking on roads where there has been an accident, but for most part, people slow down and look, not because they want to revel in the fascination of damage but to see whether the people involved are all right. Similarly, the hurt child in all of us makes us look for those who would offer us that compassion and means to healing and accompany us in the journey to healing. This points to powerful recognition of the urge to reconcile in the form of healing within the human condition. If we are strong, healthy and whole, then we should also want to protect the weak and vulnerable. Sometimes though, we fear disease and injury in others and try to stay away from them. Sometimes being healthy can feed our own egos and sense of superiority – and that can hurt others.

Marthe

When I got cancer, everyone was very kind, but some of my friends stopped calling me. They seemed to be embarrassed about it, like they didn't know what to say. Then I heard a friend's little girl say to my daughter 'Will you catch cancer from your mum?' It turned out that my friend thought it could be true. Then another time I heard my friend's daughter say 'At least *my* mum hasn't got cancer'. And that made me feel terrible, like somehow I was letting my kids down.

The healed wound typically results in a scar which is a visible sign of the reconciling process, as the body reconciles itself with its injury and repairs the damage. As time passes, most scars then fade. Yet, as we have seen, healed wounds do not mean that a person is completely unscathed. An unhealed wound is the sign of something seriously wrong, and ultimately movement towards death. This can be true of mental wounds as well as physical ones.

Christ's wounds

As we learned from Jurgen Moltmann above, the wounded Christ provides the Church with a powerful symbol of God's reconciling work on an

Unreconciled human being. As the incarnation of God in human form, Jesus experiences intense physical pain and mental anguish. His body is flogged and then nailed to a cross; his flesh is torn and broken. Yet the mangled body which was taken down in death and buried, is shown again to the disciples after the resurrection, the wounds, what has happened, are clearly visible. What has happened to Jesus is not remade as if it had never been, but transformed and brought into the experience of the divine life. What does it mean in the mission of the Church to direct people towards worship of a crucified God, whose identification with the Unreconciled leads him in Mark's account to enter into their state and transform it, 'my God, my God why have you abandoned me?' (Mark 15.34).

There can be a tendency in the Church to ignore this aspect of the resurrected Christ living in peace and glory with God but also as the one who is wounded (and/or) scarred forever by the experience of Incarnation.[1] So our life experiences, their joys and pains, are not rubbed out but can undergo change and transformation. Yet in the Church we often talk as if conversion and transformation in Christ are seen as a new start which absolves responsibility for a past life and all that has happened. The language used by some Christians of being 'born again' sometimes also presupposes the new person as tabula rasa, the old life destroyed, yet this is difficult to square with reconciliation and mission as a means to transformation which acknowledges the need to overcome evil by speaking its name and changing it.

Tara (swimming pool attendant/instructor/trainer)

If you asked me a few weeks ago I'd have said this was a good place to see reconciliation in action. It's because you get people coming to get therapy, to recover from illness, or to help with disability. Kids with special needs become themselves in the water. You see mums with babies leaving their worries at the door and really bonding with themselves and each other. You see kids having fun. You see couples enjoying being together. You see lonely people making friends. There's something about taking your clothes off and getting in the water that sets people free, even if it's only time out or time to think. People don't lie when they swim. Look at me (Tara is BIG) I have health problems, I can't run. But people don't sneer at me in a swimming costume because I am good at what I do and I can save lives. They trust me. When you're sitting and watching for problems you can see all kinds of people, all kinds of life and if there's anyone there who shouldn't be you can spot them pretty soon – they can't blend in. I help people to get over their fear of water, all ages, all walks of life can get something here. I love it when kids who can't walk are laughing together in the water. You get people who are fanatics, who do endless lengths, but that's who they are, they're owning up to something.

The tragedy [a boy drowned recently] shook all that a bit, but I still think this is good place to see reconciliation in action.

Physical wounds and mental scars can condemn different groups of people to the land of the Unreconciled and they need reconciliation through healing to allow them back into the communities where they can flourish and grow. This does not mean that every imperfection should be eradicated, it does not mean that we should run for cosmetic surgery at the first sign of wrinkles or because we don't like a blemish. The image of perfection is not behind us but in front of us – we are all waiting for the beauty.

Yet reconciling action can be offered to those who suffer wounds and bear scars and as Christians we need to support those who work in the

---

1 Debates in the tradition have continued about whether Jesus' resurrection body bears wounds or scars. Is the Lamb who is perpetually slain still bleeding?

medical profession, in hospitals and hospices and in people's homes. We need to be at the forefront of those accepting and bringing into community those who are Unreconciled because of how they look or because of what has happened to them, showing by example that they are loved and that they enrich our community. And we should be aware of those among us, such as those in military service returning from active duty, whose experiences in war torn areas need to be heard and their stories accepted. By being loving, open and reconciling communities we can provide a glimpse of that ultimate reconciling in God who will in the end receive all that we are and all that has happened to us, and who knows the secrets of all our hearts.

Otherness and Self

Metaphysical poets have often sought to describe the longing in human beings to be ultimately reconciled with the creator God. They also particularly wrote of the relationship between a person's sense of self and the beloved Other whose image resides in us and who is God. For example, Andrew Marvell's poem *On a Drop of Dew* speaks of a dewdrop longing for the sun as a human soul longs for God. Yet for the dewdrop to be reconciled with the sun, it must give up its separate existence. As a dewdrop on earth, it creates a tiny mirror of the greater reality, but at last wants to come home, and 'dissolving, run/Into the Glories of th'Almighty Sun'. Similarly, George Herbert in *Love (III)* imagines his soul as a guest at a feast, longing to join the party but feeling unworthy until Love overcomes 'dust and sin' and allows the beloved to join in the heavenly banquet. Such poets offer us a language of desire, of longing, which helps us understand that out of the Unreconciled state there is a deep spiritual impulse potentially in *everyone* towards reconciliation with the Other. We have a task in mission to recognise that language of longing and respond to that desire.

The Other

The Greek words translated 'reconciled' or 'reconciliation' in the New Testament have buried within them the root of a word meaning 'the other.' Implicit in that is what Martin Buber means when he suggests that the essence of true dialogue is a turning towards the other. That relationship between self and other lies at the heart of much of Christian theology and it is important within the mission of God's love to the world, the *missio dei*. Reconciliation, then, depends on being clear who *we* are both in our individual lives and also in our communities. We also have to know who those 'others' are with whom we would create relationships and with whom we would build the Kingdom. St Paul says that God loving us in Christ is itself a reconciling process which turns enemies into friends and so creates peace. It is a covenantal process: God loves us in Christ and we are called to reflect that in the world by making these relationships between self and other. We can see this in the Bible. One of the ethical tests for the people of Israel was their treatment of strangers and aliens among them and one of the most shocking strands in Jesus' teaching was that a good neighbour, treating a stranger as oneself, could be revealed as a despised Samaritan, the person you would cross the road to avoid..

Yet although we can be keenly aware of the longing to be reconciled with the Other who is God and know that it our task as Christians to be reconciled with other people, the task is neither straightforward nor easy.

As Alison Webster puts it:

'Ask yourself this question: who is my other? Who or what springs to mind? Is it someone you distrust, are intimidated by, cannot relate to? Is it someone or a group that is strange to you, that you do not immediately understand? Or is the 'otherness' about how the logic of this life fits together, that is not yours? Is it his motivations and values –about what makes him do as he does? Or is it more basic than that? Is it his outward appearance and all that you associate with it – the ghosts of your past exerting an influence in the present?'[1]

When a group of teenagers were asked to consider Alison's question, the kind of ideas they came up with were: the way we walk around the homeless

1 Alison Webster, op.cit., p.31

person on the street or, the way we move seats to avoid the person talking to herself. Or how we might find the person with heavy make up and piercings intimidating or even feeling wary of a group of different teenagers standing around at a street corner. On further discussion, however, it was clear that the 'other' also can also be part of a group we call 'self': the person who comes to church but nobody talks to, the boy at school everybody avoids because he's 'strange', the step-sister the rest of the siblings never include in their games or outings.

So the task of building relationships between self and other depends on facing honestly the problems we ourselves have with 'others' around us and finding out what it takes to repair broken relationships in our own communities. How do we treat our own – the poor, the voiceless, or as below, the disabled child in a competitive, success driven society?

Karen (football development instructor)

One of the things I think I know about is how people do or don't fit in. When people come here, it's often because they've got a parent who thinks their son is gong to be the next David Beckham, they're ambitious to the extent of annihilating anyone else who gets in their way. When they get here, the kids have to learn how to get on with one another as a team. It doesn't matter how good you are, you have to learn co-operation. So kids who have the idea of fame and fortune dangled in front of them have to give that up for team playing and team skills. Parents have to think again about what this business of football has to do with them. Some of them don't like it, but most of them come round. A lot of the dads have to realise that their child is never going to develop as a striker, the glory merchant, but as the defender who is every bit as important. They have to see a bigger picture.

In my own life I had to make a decision about Anna (her daughter) because she is deaf. She is not so deaf that she couldn't go to a mainstream school but I sent her (to a school for children with special needs) because there she isn't different, even though all the children have different abilities and requirements. It's a community where she's teaching everyone else and learning from everyone else. She's special in a place where everyone is special. She doesn't live in a target driven environment. She does well at school, but that's not what matters. It's reconciled, but it's not second best. It's second better if you know what I mean.

Alienation

The teenagers realised that even within our own familiar web of relationships and connections, we can alienate people and reduce them to an Unreconciled state which can get worse the longer it goes on. With the advent of global mobility, and political changes such as the expansion of the European Union, we see more and more issues arising in respect of our behaviour towards asylum seekers, refugees, communities such as travellers and gypsies and the influx of economic migrants. All of these people can be designated Other and denied integration and hospitality. When this happens they become the Unreconciled ones and may face having to overcome that label in everything they then try to do. Conversely, some of these groups may themselves resist integration because they feel that being drawn into the community will compromise their language, culture or history. This raises the question: how can we offer Christian hospitality and friendship to people without making them feel like we are trying to assimilate them, change them or convert them against their will?

Meriel, traveller

When we came to this area, people were cross with us because they said we were trespassing and that we made a mess everywhere. Then some people came and said the children should be in this or that school and if they didn't have the medicine they would get ill. When we went into the shop we were told to get out. Some other people turned up and tried to take the ponies away. That's when the police came.

We've got stories we tell the children and we know how to look after them. We've always lived this way. We look after our animals. We're people and we're happy. (Meriel was told not to say any more.)

Sometimes we put people into an Unreconciled category and sometimes people find it easier and safer to live there, fearing what we might do to them otherwise. Why does this happen? Jesus drew condemnation for crossing powerful invisible barriers giving him access to taboo and forbidden Others such as prostitutes, outcasts, lepers and sinners. This reckless breaking of religious and societal rules frightened and scandalised people. We cannot follow Jesus' example, unless we understand what is at the bottom of this fear and concern in the community of 'self'. For many people, fear of the Other stems from insecurity and fear of attack or change. It is sometimes expressed as resentment when Others do not appear to live by the same conventions, rules or language. The argument 'if they want to live in this country, they should live like us' is often heard in relation to diet, religion, and conventions of dress. Another argument is that Others use up resources which are needed for the dominant community. Asylum seekers and refugees need goods and services which our own are also struggling for. Another fear is that Others will usurp what we are striving for – they will take our jobs, remove our wealth and offer us nothing in return. For example, refugees are often alienated from their homelands; they are dispossessed and have nowhere to go and therefore need our love and shelter. But they may appear to others as 'cuckoos' looking to push out someone else in their search for a resting place. For asylum seekers too there is a sense of rejection and exclusion, which can be profound. For such people there can be a profound sense of isolation, as they are rejected by one culture, but then not accepted by another. They may feel they have no location or place on earth. They are removed from society and become even more Unreconciled.

Sometimes it is felt Others will place huge burdens on our communities, dragging them down, the story behind Meriel's words above, which from the community's point of view is a picture of the travellers leaving rubbish and damage to public land which clean up cost gets passed on to council tax payers. Such perceptions fuel resentment and fear and create a climate of desire to expel the Other from our midst. But what is often not articulated is the fact that we don't have the desire, motivation or mechanisms to engage the Other effectively.

Jacintha, community liaison

My job involves sorting out problems to do with the travellers and gypsies who move around the area. What I want is to make it possible for the different communities to live in peace, but the travellers create a lot of negative feeling wherever they go. They create outrage in the community on three fronts, children, animals and rubbish. We've got problems with them dumping their children and disappearing, often in shops, or in church, or in public amenities and expecting them to be taken care of. We've got problems with animals wandering on the roads and getting hurt. And the worst problem is public outrage at the tipping and rubbish that nobody wants to clear away. Reconciliation is a problem with different groups of people recognising different boundaries. Wrong perceptions pile up: travellers don't' love their children, don't care for their animals and are generally dirty. None of these things are true. Because their boundaries are different, people think they have no respect for personal property and must be criminals. There was outrage when they camped in the Tesco's car park, with people assuming that they were raiding the supermarket, but in fact that never happened. Travellers are often the victims of crime. Reconciliation for me means getting rid of the myths and trying to find practical means for everyone to live in peace.

> Two children from a refugee family had a difficult time at school and were perpetually bullied. One day, the class read a story in an English lesson called *Refugee Boy*. After discussion in the class, some of the children asked the two refugee children about their own past and realised that their own stories were just as harrowing. After this there was no more bullying and the children were voted to receive a school award for overcoming difficulties. They went from being pariahs to being celebrated.

Getting the stories of other communities among us accepted and heard can be very difficult where resentment and fear causes incredible deafness.

So reconciliation for mission requires addressing this fear and creating a safe space for mutual encounter to take place. This necessarily requires willingness by those we think of as Other to participate and to hear the fears and concerns without arrogance or rancour. It is worth also remembering that we are 'Other' to them also. We see this in John 4 with the story of Jesus' conversation with the Samaritan woman at the well. If Samaritans were Other to Jews, Jews were also certainly Other to Samaritans, and the problems with overcoming this is clear from the woman's questions; 'How is it that you, a Jew, ask a drink of me, a woman of Samaria'. Both Jesus and the woman have work to do if their encounter is to be meaningful and give birth to new possibilities.

The alienated Christian

One important theological question concerns how we as Christians relate to the society and cultures in which we live. A thorny mission question is whether by engaging fully in our modern culture we our selling out to its consumerist mores, or whether Christian faith and church life should be essentially counter-cultural, perpetually challenging Others outside the church with the vision of a living, alternative community. Also, as Britain changes and becomes more multicultural Christian congregations may find themselves in a minority in some areas. The Presence and Engagement process provides support and resources to such Christian congregations who are now at the forefront of thinking about what kinds of reconciling initiatives can be made to enable communities to live together peacefully and how Christian faith can be witnessed to and shared with others sensitively. See www.presenceandengagement.org.uk

Prisoners of conscience

Following on from this, there might be times when Christians find it necessary to resist a reconciling of Self and Other when the result of that reconciliation would be to compromise our understanding of God's will for the world. We believe in reconciling processes which lead to the world becoming more like what God wants but there are of course regimes, cultures and processes which we need to resist, including those which seek to suppress religious conviction and expressions of worship. Prisoners of conscience are often alienated from their dominant cultures because they have made a choice to be reconciled with their own inner being rather than submit to belief or behaviour that they think is contrary to the gospel. Becoming a prisoner of conscience is a protest against the Other who refuses the vision of the Kingdom of God. The crucifixion prompts us to ask whether Jesus can also be considered a prisoner of conscience. On the cross he suffers alienation, but this allows our reconciliation with God.

Simon Beer's candle reminds us that some forms of alienation are deliberately embraced in order to show forth a greater hope. So the candle

shines steadily and brightly within the encircling spikes and barbed wire. So when Christians resist absorption or refuse to compromise their faith in order to join the dominant culture it can be a powerful form of witness. This does not have to happen in some vast global arena, it can occur for example in work environments where people are asked to behave in ways their Christian faith finds unacceptable, such as circulating racist or pornographic material, or persecuting homosexuals or people of other faiths.

Peacemaking

The reconciliation of Self and Other perhaps becomes most acute in situations where there is war. All kinds of problems need to be addressed before something new can be forged between the warring factions or countries. For example, war can entrench appalling divisions between the different parties, so that there is no common ground on which to move forward. This may be made even more problematic where we are involved in other countries and peacemaking or peacekeeping can be complicated by a sense of our own superior position, or identification with victimised people and their legitimate concerns. It is sometimes easier to stereotype people and dehumanize them, in the theatre of war, designating them only as 'the enemy'. We may also approach the issue of reconciliation with suspicion and a readiness to believe the worst and then react to feedback by only accepting that which confirms our worst fears. At its most extreme, we may come to demonize the Other in a way which eclipses their essential humanity completely. And of course, the Other may approach us in exactly the same way. Some soldiers in Afghanistan have reported the difficulties of engaging with local populations who must be kept at a distance for fear of attack. Offers of friendship and kindness must all be treated with suspicion and regard for personal safety first. Soldiers say that living like this leads to a distorted sense of reality and the constant refusal of relationship and culture of suspicion is extremely wearing and difficult to maintain.

Ryung Suh, US Army Flight Surgeon

How will we separate the enemies from innocent civilians? When an aviator in an Apache helicopter sees an Afghan man walking away from an explosion site with two sheep in tow, is he observing a sheepherder or an Al Qaeda attacker? We've dropped bombs on Taliban targets whose cellular phones direct our hit and, consequently, we've had to deal with unintended civilian deaths. We have Afghan civilians building our volleyball courts and hauling our trash, knowing that many relay critical operational information to our enemies (some were caught using mirrors to guide in rocket attacks).[1]

It can be difficult and disorienting to consider that in the minds of others we can be 'the enemy' and can appear as threatening and hostile demons to those we would seek to engage in dialogue and transformational change. From the other side, there may be a perception that the only way to get us to take notice is by force. We know what this feels like to *us* when we

---

1 Online at http://www.soldiertestimony.org/wordpress/?cat=86

watch the bright ball of flame issue from the World Trade Centre or open our newspapers to pictures of a smashed and wrecked bus on the streets of London. But can we ever imagine what landscapes of thought existed in the imagination of the bombers before they blew themselves to pieces? We talk about 'radicalisation' and about terrorism, but what is that really like in the life of a human being, what is its language, what *colour* is it?

Canon Andrew White

The difficulties of peacemaking are very real. It may sound wonderful but it is always difficult and often dangerous. I do not know how many times I have been shot at, hijacked and had doors slammed in my face. I live with a price on my head and often I am prevented from doing what I want to and need to do by my security in Baghdad. The difficulties of being a peacemaker are real and often prevent people from pursuing the reality of this calling. It is difficult but our Lord calls us to do it. 'Blessed are the peacemakers for they shall be called the children of G-d.' [1]

This reminds us that reconciliation work in a world torn by war and oppression will not stand up to platitudes or niceness. The Unreconciled people who have to be engaged in the process of reconciliation and peacemaking initiatives may not be 'nice'. Canon White wrote that they were without doubt people who have been involved in 'war, chaos, terrorism and disaster. They are the kind of people involved in kidnapping, blowing up buses and hurting the often innocent. There is little rationality and no secrets in how to get them to change'. But God asks us to get to know them and like Jonah, we are required to face a task that may seem utterly daunting and frightening. The command to love our enemies from Jesus does not have an identical concept in either Islam or Judaism, so this is a reconciliatory path that must be forged by Christians. Conversely, we may have to remember that Christianity has in its own history a great deal of violence in the name of a religious ideal, violence which we now want to repudiate and reject. Why we do so and how we can repent of past violence informs the way we now set against violence which goes on in the name of religion today.

We may easily forget the tension and stress of such work, but the rewards are not necessarily huge changes, peace agreements or ceasefires, but very small things which matter just as much to God. Andrew White points to rays of hope: 'a Sunna and Shia cleric share a meal together or a hostage is returned. Suddenly hope is returned. A hope that is often far more theological than political. Often the politics give very little hope and then unexpectedly the hope of the resurrection breaks through. I think of the days when all has seemed so bleak in the Middle East that I have gone to the

---

1 Personal letter to MTAG from Canon Andrew White, President of the Foundation for Relief and Reconciliation in the Middle East.

empty tomb of Christ and just stood there. The empty tomb has been what has spurred me on.'

The *motivation* for Christians to keep going in this difficult peacemaking is very important, because we cannot get involved in the reconciliation of Self with Other unless our motivation and strength to continue is linked inextricably with God's intention and with what God has done in Christ. Just as Canon White tells us about the hope represented by the paradox of the empty tomb, so he also tells us of the suffering and rewards.

> I have on several occasions sat with my staff in Baghdad and cried at the news of disaster and death which we have tried to prevent. This kind of peacemaking is painful, difficult, time consuming and at the same time wonderful. I will never forget the time when two of my close colleagues were with me at a press conference in London. One was a Rabbi and member of the Israeli Parliament, the other was an Islamic Sheik and member of the Palestinian Legislative Assembly. An Arab journalist soon started to attack the Sheik for working with the Rabbi.... the sheik took the rabbi's hand and said 'Rabbi Melchior is my brother and I will walk the path of reconciliation with him until we find peace'. He was then asked what he (thought) he (was) doing and he answered 'I am pulling up the thorns on the path and planting flowers'. ...It is days like this one that give me hope and enable me to continue, knowing that people can change.

This story reflects the exopsition of the story of Jacob and Esau by Israel Selvanayagam, when he says that 'The key (to reconciliation) is seeing the face of God in one's brother's face, particularly when that brother remains a longstanding victim of exploitation and injustice'.[1] David Ford also asks: 'might it even be that justice is rooted in the face to face?'[2] Reconciliation for mission then, is not an easy thing to get involved with. It is not a matter of representing what Christians 'stand for' or improving the public profile of the Church. It is in fact a requirement that we adopt all the characteristics of Jesus that so appalled and frightened people, when he broke taboos, enraged the authorities and put himself and his disciples in danger. Reaching out to the Unreconciled, standing before them face to face, and birthing a new thing on God's behalf is risky business. It can tear us apart. In offering Mary the opportunity to bring Christ into the world, she was told the reality of the situation: 'a sword will pierce your own soul, too' (Luke 2.35).

---

1 Israel Selvanayagam, 'Gal-ed versus Peniel: True reconciliation in the Esau-Jacob/Israel story' in Kirsteen Kim (ed), (2005) *Reconciling Mission: The Ministry of Healing and Reconciliation in the Church Worldwide* (Delhi: ISPCK)

2 David Ford, (1999) *Self and Salvation, being transformed*, (Cambridge: Cambridge University Press) p. 20 and see in context in the whole chapter on 'Facing'.

Separation and Unity

The unseen Unreconciled

When we talk about reconciliation we tend to think of parties which are separated by some obvious problem, whether it is countries at war, or two people on the brink of divorce. In such situations the gap between them is obvious and acts of reconciliation try to close that gap and bring reparations, peace-making and conflict resolution.

However, there are also communities where no such obvious conflicts exist. Such communities may live apparently happily side by side, co-existing without difficulty, but right in the heart of such communities, even between neighbours, there can be a deep layer of the Unreconciled state which is never talked about or questioned.

Such communities may be divided by different understandings of their shared history. The narrative of history, written by the powerful, written by victors, is heard louder and fiercer, but the other voices are never truly silenced. Where these different voices continue to speak side by side, with neither engagement nor communication, they nurture not a potentially creative sense of individuality and difference, but fault lines of suspicion and competition which, at their most extreme, give vent one day to ethnic cleansing and genocide. A shared history of past conflict that is never properly examined can reside deep in the psyche and break out in violent conflict when present inequalities or injustices are seen to be reproducing the power relations imposed by past struggles – even where communities have seemingly lived in peace for many years. In some cases of deep-seated historical injustice, work has been done extensively to expose this underlying damage and to put processes in place to heal memories and breaches. This has been done with the Holocaust, with the Truth and Reconciliation Commission (TRC) in South Africa and also with public apologies by religious institutions and governments for slavery, collusion, land seizure and forced adoption. But elsewhere, the difficulties remain unexamined and never really go away.

Examples of such Unreconciled communities can include different cultures and ethnicities which live side by side, or different religions which live side by side. Such communities may appear to live peaceably together, respecting each other's space and independence while also engaging in friendly interchange. In such cases, it often takes a flashpoint, even a trivial one, to reveal the deeply entrenched positions and the extent of the divide. A banner in a window, a gesture by a footballer on the pitch, graffiti on a wall – all of these can be sparks which become flames. Sometimes, then,

Christians seek to move forward in mission, but then find it difficult to progress where unseen divisions and unhealed hurts exist just beneath the surface. In some cases well-meaning Christian outreach can unwittingly fan the flames. In exploring moves towards the reconciling work at the heart of mission, this reminds us that we must also listen to darker, sadder stories and come to know something of the shadowed and unfinished side of the spiritual journey, in which you believe your heavenly reward is to see your enemies get hammered. There are powerful spiritual and psychological feelings involved in seeing the people you resent get their just desserts; it can be the underlying current beneath the concept of 'vindication'. And sometimes this perspective continues to run on and on through apparently quiet towns and villages.

We might assume that Unreconciled communities are most apparent in the global arena, but in fact, they may be present among us too. In the UK, there are many examples of the Unreconciled which challenge our assumptions about reconciliation and mission. We look below at Northern Ireland and at Wales.

Northern Ireland

In Northern Ireland, political moves towards reconciliation have been welcomed by many, but beneath the surface, there are still difficulties in enabling Catholics and Protestants to live within each other's communities. Estate agents have often thought of Belfast in terms of 'green' or 'orange' areas and noted how some areas, such as West Belfast have changed their colour over time. When this happens the remaining 'green' or 'orange' inhabitants, especially those who cannot afford to move out, begin to feel more threatened, and the thoughts and feelings of the Unreconciled communities rise to the surface.

Marching season remains a recognised flashpoint. Those Protestants who march insist it is part of their culture and tradition; those Catholics in the communities through which the marches occur often see the events as inflammatory and provocative. Each year, in marching season, underlying tensions are tested again. When the Unreconciled issues erupt into violence sometimes only part of the whole story is told. For example in the protests at the Roman Catholic Holy Cross School in 2001and 2002, the media focused on the problems faced by the children being unable to get to class, but it was not reported that Protestant senior citizens had earlier been attacked on their way to the Post Office. Holy Cross became a focus of a series of incidents in the area and was an instance of a threatened community reacting, and which like an unquiet volcano, could continue to erupt as was seen in 2003:

> The Holy Cross dispute had calmed down in recent months but was never formally or finally settled, with tensions never far from the surface. Loyalists have remained unhappy about

Catholic pupils going into their district, but had accepted that their protest was counter-productive and harmful to their cause. There has been little recent evidence of a fresh groundswell of militancy among local Protestants, but the UDA has shown it has the capacity to whip up ill-feeling. What is not clear is whether the pipe bomb attack is an isolated incident or the start of a series of loyalist protests.[1]

In addition, David Porter one of the members of the Consultative Group of the Past (Eames-Bradley Report 2009) told a meeting at St Ethelburga's Peace and Reconciliation Centre that he had heard terrible stories of how rifts and tensions are perpetuated in the community. He told the story of bereaved families who receive letters or phone calls on the anniversary of the death of their loved ones, from perpetrators who use the occasion to gloat over what they have done. In such a situation, the families cannot move on or allow time to heal their wounds because others continue to make sure the wounds stay open.

Despite a huge amount of reconciliation work, there are still problems with addressing the gulf that remains between different Christians and for some of those Christians, who have no sacramental mechanism for asking for forgiveness and reconciliation, there may literally be no language that will enable them to move forward. There is regret, certainly, but in traditions which look forward to God as final judge, that future accounting cannot impact on hurt fellow Christians who need to hear the good news of repentance and transformation *now*. When there are non-existent or conflicting mechanisms for repentance and healing this can result in others carrying more of the blame rising up from the Unreconciled tensions in the community. For example, the police in Northern Ireland ended up being a kind of third community with examples of policemen being banned in their own churches from taking communion.

David Porter suggested to us that the task is: 'what is God saying to us in this mess?'[2] What does the gospel say to a context of conflict? It is naïve for Christians to assume that our longing for the Kingdom will always easily supersede all other forms of belonging. In such a situation the Kingdom is all very well, but we have to face the realities of communities which have been abandoned by government and beset by terrorism. For people on the ground, there is frustration with 'professional theology' which does not embody itself in the realities of living in these communities. If, for example, theological

---

1 David McKittrick, 'Holy Cross pipe bomb raises fear that loyalists may revive dispute', *The Independent*, 7th January 2003.

2 David Porter spoke to us at length on this issue at a MTAG residential in Belfast. One response is the setting up of Contemporary Christianity in Ireland [formerly ECONI]. ECONI originally came into existence to resist the elements which were subverting Christian identity. ECONI tried to restore a perspective of working for God and his glory and set out a statement of 10 biblical principles to challenge evangelicals to rethink what being Christian means in this context. See www.contemporarychristianity.org.

education does not equip people to work among the Unreconciled, progress is very difficult to achieve, especially as so many clergy coming into such situations encounter paralysing chunks of blame. Even when life seems to be peaceful, without being aware and involved with the tensions of Unreconciled communities, we cannot hope for life on earth to be as it is in heaven.

How then, are clergy and laity to be equipped to find the wounds beneath the surface of communities? One important issue is that of land and location, developing an understanding of where people live and what those locations mean to people.[1] This is true in every community but especially in communities where there is, or has been, conflict. Geographical elements often make a difference. In Northern Ireland the conflict and experience of the Troubles is different in every valley, but of course the Peace Process, as a political process, cannot acknowledge this variation in shared memory and experience; like all political solutions it tends to assume that there is one overarching experience for everybody. But for someone living in mainly Protestant East Belfast, life looks and feels different from the experience of another person living in mainly Catholic West Belfast, on top of which development and urbanisation are continuing to change these communities. Before reconciliation can even be thought of, we have to ask: what does it mean to belong there?

Against this background, middle class people continue to move around because they can afford to do so. As this happens, unreconciled tensions cause the communities to polarise and set up a form of religious apartheid. Where Belfast has Catholics areas, Protestants form satellite communities. Economic migration within the city continues to drive two communities each with their own clubs and leisure facilities. The divisions between the communities are continued in segregated schooling which has consequences for the education and nurture of Christians on both sides of the divide. There is no sense of how there could be one community, so Kingdom values make little sense, instead there is a need to address the wounds beneath the surface. Finding an appropriate way to do that however, has itself caused contention and become a source of anger. For example, the recommendations in the Eames-Bradley report, including a controversial compensation payment of £12,000 for each family which had suffered a death in the Troubles, including those of dead paramilitaries, received majority opposition through the public consultations. [2] The objections spelled out many unresolved issues about victimhood, continuing suffering, the need to bring enemies to account and suspicion of measures to 'solve' continuing problems. However recommendation 15 of the report, which suggested working with the churches, generated this response:

---

1 To think about this, see for example, Louise Lawrence (2009) *The Word in Place: Reading the New Testament in Contemporary Contexts* (London: SPCK).

2 The results were published 19th July 2010. Available online at http://www.cvsni.org/ images/stories/dealing_past/nio_summary_responses_to_cgp_consultation.pdf.

Many respondents who supported this proposal emphasised the importance of the role the Churches in Northern Ireland in promoting a non-sectarian future. The Methodist Church in Ireland noted that they took 'this challenge very seriously' and highlighted the 'need to spell out what Christian reconciliation looks like' The Church of Ireland Working Group's response outlined the significant amount of work they had already undertaken in this area and noted that it is 'ready to make an ongoing contribution'. The Peacemaking Group of the Belmont Presbyterian Church and the Quakers were also strongly supportive of the Churches engaging on these issues.[1]

The will is clearly manifest in the churches to make a difference. So we have to ask how it is possible to give leadership and to shape the spiritual life of the community. The churches have been complicit in the past; now a prophetic voice is needed, including the voice lament for the Unreconciled condition which is so evident from the public responses to the report.

David Porter tells us:

> In general what you see recommended is toleration and accommodation. It is not reconciliation at all. Reconciliation is actually rare. The dysfunctional problems of identity map on to eschatological thinking. Power belongs to God. Identity is found in God. So what can we do? Protestants bear witness to the overcoming of violence only after death. The eschatological reality is that we come to die. But the Church is living in denial of our own human experience of people dying, living and escaping.

Speaking about the £12,000 payment proposal, David Porter emphasised that death and bereavement hurt all families equally and so there was an attempt to acknowledge that shared pain in the Bradley-Eames report. Yet it is clear that this 'reconciling' offer cannot address the chasms of Unreconciled experience and feeling; that the victims and the victimised are not equal in death; that compensation or recognition will not touch pain.

Raymond Elliott, present at the Shankhill bombing

Money can never bring back what's happened. Plus Eames and Bradley have never seen the mess that a bomb can cause. You have to be there to understand.[2]
. . . .

As Christians we need to know what more we can do than address the heartbreaking mess, the continuing echoes of the bombings. What can emerge that is new?

---

1 Ibid, p. 24.
2 Quoted at http://www.u.tv/news/Public-reject-Troubles-legacy-report/ d0f1bc65-8636-443b-b7d1-15b47d414de7.

Wales

What might reconciliation, rather than 'toleration and accommodation' look like in places where actual conflict is long past? The six hundredth anniversary of the last attempt by a Welsh prince to gain 'home rule' by armed rising was commemorated in Wales in 2004 but does six hundred years without conflict mean reconciliation? Many places in the world today would be overjoyed to have such a history of peace and if 'toleration and accommodation' can produce not only six hundred years without violence between specific communities but a shared space without even the threat of violence, ought we not be satisfied with that? Biblical peace is a positive quality though, not simply the absence of conflict. In Wales, we see that reconciliation is hindered not only by conscious hostility and prejudice but also from differing understanding of common concepts.

Anwen

They were nice people who bought the cottage in the village but they lived in Birmingham. They said, 'We like the summers but it's too cold in the winter'. I said 'but in the winter you still see everybody and everyone pulls together. It's really nice. When the stable building fell down because of the snow, we all helped put it back up again, even the kids. They said 'Exactly. It's far too cold in the winter.' They just don't get it, living here.

In Wales, the Cymru-Cymraeg, (those Welsh-speaking and born in Wales) for the most part live peaceably with their English speaking neighbours and indeed with those living and working among them from England and elsewhere. But there continues to be reports about incidents where English people buying second homes in the Welsh countryside, or boats on the coast, have had their property destroyed. Such incidents have often been reported as political acts: the result of Welsh people acting to protect the Welsh language and culture. But if we dig deeper beyond the overt cause, we come to misunderstandings and confusions about the idea of home and belonging which feeds the Unreconciled condition of the communities living alongside one another. There often persists the sense that, while English neighbours are made welcome and find a valued role within the community, their belonging, their home, is somewhere else.

> It became known that one of the partners of the local veterinary practice was approaching retirement. He had worked in the practice for the majority of his working life. He and his wife had lived in the same village all that time and brought up their family there. Local people liked and respected them. Their children had attended the village primary school and spoke Welsh.. They were both originally from South Wales. As the time for his retirement drew near, his wife was asked whether they would be 'going home'.

This is not the result of historical antagonism to descendents of former enemies but a different view of what it means to belong, a misunderstanding probably common to the interfaces between rural and urban communities everywhere. The indigenous Welsh speaking communities of Wales have always had to leave to find work but they still know where their home is. Some people make their living in England or elsewhere but come back to their family roots as retirement approaches. Home is not somewhere you make wherever you choose but is the place to which you *ultimately* belong, a focal point for all your networks, roots and memories. So to buy a home to which you don't belong not only deprives those for whom that place really *is* home, it also has something of an insult about it, not just in terms of material wealth or property, but of undermining what it means to belong.

It is assumed that people who come to live and work in rural Wales from elsewhere will also have a home elsewhere to which they belong and to which they may very well return. So the enquiry about going home is not a rejection, even if it feels like one, but a question about your wellbeing, your need to get back to where your heart is.

> The very first question a Welsh learner is taught to ask in one well-used Welsh language course is, "Where do you come from originally?"

So the desire of rootless urban incomers to belong to the rural communities into which they come can be frustrated by the indigenous assumption that everyone belongs where they come from. But just because you don't 'belong' because your heart is assumed to be elsewhere, doesn't mean you're not welcome. In this perspective, the host community recognises the incomers as Unreconciled because they are away from their origins and needs to make space for them. But this in turn challenges the newcomers to learn to be honoured and welcomed strangers. How can we learn to be strangers, when we all want to feel we 'belong' wherever we go? Philippians 3.20 reminds us that we are all citizens of heaven and so even our lives on earth are as it were in temporary accommodation while we wait to return to where we truly belong. As part of the hospitality of the Kingdom, do we assume that we will be in charge, in control, or do we have to pay better attention to what it means to be adopted, to be guests in God's house?

Another issue in the rift of Unreconciled concerns between communities in Wales centres around language, especially when native English speakers, whether Welsh people or English, move into Welsh speaking Wales. Language is a vehicle of culture and a marker of identity but in the first place, it simply *is*. People speak first the language their parents speak. Misunderstandings arise when English speakers assume that when Welsh people, who are also fluent in English, speak Welsh to one another, they are making a political point rather than simply speaking their native tongue, the language in which they think and feel. Perhaps native English speakers, one of the very few monoglot communities in the world, are more sensitive than other language groups might be. People who have recently moved into rural Welsh towns from the new accession countries of the EU are keen to try out their recently acquired Welsh alongside the English which they also have to learn.

Many of those who move into Welsh speaking rural Wales do try to learn the language, something that is greatly appreciated by the Welsh speaking community. It enables community life to be continued in the local language and enables incomers to take part in and understand more of the life of the community in which they live. But without sensitivity, even such positive gestures can become a spearhead for the ultimate cultural imperialism, the sense that the language of your thoughts and feelings, the language of your sense of home, can be appropriated and changed by others for whom the words are not tied to generations of lived experience.

Jo Penberthy

I was taking part in a Confirmation service at a neighbouring parish church. I had taken two young people to be confirmed by the Bishop. The service was conducted in both English and Welsh. As I looked around the congregation, it struck me that while almost everyone sitting in the pews was a native Welsh speaker, not one of the four robed people standing at front helping to take the service was. Three were English people, all with various degrees of fluency in Welsh and the other was me, Welsh born and bred but only a Welsh learner. I had a sudden horrid vision of well meaning English urban people, fluent in Welsh, becoming the leaders all over rural Welsh speaking Wales.

Even if you use the same words you might never see with the same eyes. You can speak like a native speaker, but it will take sensitivity and a willingness to listen and learn to be able to appreciate how to hear and think like a native speaker, to love language rather than merely use it as a tool of communication.

Cultural sensitivity is therefore difficult and a lack of it feeds the Unreconciled condition. The need to develop sensitivity is made more complex by the power differentials between the two groups of Welsh-speaking and English-speaking people. If we argue that reconciling action can only come about between equals, then in Wales there are problems not only of language but of political and economic power. English is spoken across the world and is the major international language of commerce and academia: Welsh, although on the increase, is spoken by a minority of Welsh people and its heartlands are areas into which inward migration of non-speakers is increasing. The presence and vibrancy of the language in political life and in the media is increasing but this inward migration is still a threat to the future of the language. Although Wales now has a devolved government, language still remains the backbone of Welsh identity. In May 2010, the appointment of an MP for an English constituency, Cheryl Gillan, as Secretary of State for Wales, was criticised as insensitive and inappropriate.[1]

How can we address the things which lie between these groups of Unreconciled in towns and villages in Wales? Reconciliation, as opposed to 'toleration' or 'accommodation' requires us to talk about what we each understand by being at 'home' and to look at ideas of belonging we may have in common. It means taking the time to find out 'what does my presence say to people around me? What assumptions do these others have about me?' To move out of the Unreconciled state requires honesty and the creation of space for listening to others' telling of their history. Reconciling bridges are built when peoples who have a history of conflict can begin to tell similar stories about that shared history. English people can find it hard to make sense of both welcome and resentment: they are welcomed in Wales and Welsh and English people intermarry, but English people rarely fail to be surprised and a little hurt as they realise that Welsh people amongst whom they live most amicably will support very vocally any team who play against England (except in cricket). They also find it hard to hear quite how resented traditional English hegemony is and fail to see themselves as part of the colonising power in their relationship with Wales. On the other hand, Welsh people often collude, not bringing these issues out into the open, rehearsing their strength of feeling amongst themselves. Many people hope that the new political settlement offers hope for reconciliation, a re-forging of Welsh identity to include all those who live within its borders but honesty about the history that has formed Welsh people is necessary to allow an Unreconciled people to transcend past inequalities. This means that there is still an underlying concern that reconciliation for the Unreconciled really means absorption of what it means to be Welsh into the dominant English order, rather than a lifting up and honouring of Welsh identity. This fear means that even biblical models of reconciliation, such as that laid out in Ephesians 2, can seem to point to an affirmation that difference and identity can be lost in pursuit of the greater wholeness: 'one humanity in place of the two, thus making peace' (2.15). For many Welsh people, addressing the Unreconciled condition means exploring further the honoured place that the Bible allots to the stranger who does not have to belong in order to be welcome and valued.

The Unreconciled on the world stage

In other situations, as we have seen more tragically in the global arena, communities living in the same land or even side by side as neighbours can erupt into implacable hatred and desire for extermination. In Bosnia and in various African countries torn by civil war, groups of people of whatever tribe or religion have been persecuted, driven from their homes, and also killed.

---

1 Originally reported at: http://www.walesonline.co.uk/cardiffonline/cardiff-news/2010/05/13/new-welsh-secretary-gillan-dismisses-criticisms-91466-26435609.

We saw above that some models of mission tend to assume that mission can overcome history, memory and even cultural and religious identity: 'There is no longer Jew or Greek, there is no longer slave or free, there is no longer male and female, for all of you are one in Jesus Christ' (Galatians 3.28). But where this understanding is used to try to overcome long standing Unreconciled communities, it can also be translated into negative emotions of hatred or fear and realised as the exercise of power. Reconciling action, then, has to undo the power imbalance, release and dissipate the negative emotions and not simply establish peace, but create something entirely new, in which the old Unreconciled identities are transmuted into shared under-standing and where each community takes responsibility for the difference and difficulty it has harboured.

The two Koreas [1]

Our desire is unification
In our dreams, our desire is unification
With all our effort, unification
Oh, come, unification!
Unification which saves our people
Unification which saves this nation
Come, unification!
Oh, come, unification! (Korean children's song) [2]

The Unreconciled people in North and South Korea exist because of a three-year war which killed over two-and-a-half million soldiers and three-and-a-half million civilians. In the process three million refugees were created and over ten million families were driven apart. Both parties committed killings, torture and kidnappings demonising each other as 'communist aggressors' or 'collaborators of the American imperialists'. The results of the war, especially the bombing of North Korea, has therefore done appalling damage to people's hearts and minds and has created deep and lasting resentments. Reconciliation attempts have to deal with profound memories of cruelty and pain across the divisions of several generations. Reunification of the two Koreas is therefore a matter which occupies all Koreans, especially those who have been separated from family members. Therefore in this arena, reconciliation is bound up with the ideological and political processes which can lead to reunification. For Christians, the question is what models of faith and action actually make sense of progress towards the goal reunification.

As Sebastian Kim notes, Korean Christian faith is intertwined with political ideas. Christians had negative attitudes toward communist ideology for a long time because of persecution of churches by the North Korean government and a general hostility to religion. So Christians have been at the forefront of anti-communist movements. In addition to positioning Christianity over against communism, theological reflection on the war also led Christians to see the war as a punishment of God toward Korean Christians for unfaithfulness. Such unfaithfulness included giving in to Japanese pressure to practise Shinto worship and was also manifested in the many divisions among the Christians themselves. Yet others understood the war as part of a sacrifice that had to take place for the greater good of the nation in line with the sacrifice of Christ for human beings. Theological reflection of this kind gave a salvific perspective to what had

---

1 The material on which this section is based was provided to us by Sebastian Kim who subsequently published it in the chapter cited below which is recommended to readers for a fuller treatment and understanding of the Unreconciled in the two Koreas.

2 Quoted in Sebastian Kim 'Reconciliation Possible? The Churches Efforts towards the Peace and Reunification of North and South Korea' in Sebastian C H Kim, Pauline Kollontai, Greg Hoyland (eds) *Peace and Reconciliation: In Search of Shared Identity* (2008) pp. 161–78.

happened in war. But the strongest perspective from Christians in the South, interpreting the war through theological eyes, was that the war had come about because of communist aggression which needed a strong Christian response, including prayer for, and mission to, the people of North Korea. The Christian response saw the evangelisation of North Korea as a first priority, creating a new landscape. Only in this new landscape would reunification be possible.

But this perspective, as a reflection on, and response to war, creates a problem, because this attitude casts mission work as the imposition of a superior ideology which itself wipes out the claims and processes of any other way of living. Reconciliation for the Unreconciled then becomes identified with imperialistic notions of what it means to be Christian.

> We confess that throughout the history of our national division the churches of Korea have not only remained silent and continuously ignored the ongoing stream of movements for autonomous reunification of our people, but have further sinned by trying to justify the division. The Christians of both North and South have made absolute idols of the ideologies enforced by their respective systems. This is a betrayal of the ultimate sovereignty of God (Exodus 20.3–5), and is a sin, for the church must follow the will of God rather than the will of any political regime (Acts 4.19).[1]

Han

Han is the word given to describe the pain and anguish felt by Koreans at what has happened in their history and specifically describes their Unreconciled state. Consequently an important function of reconciliation for mission is the overcoming of *han*. Those who are victims of a divided Korea are called Minjung and Minjung theologians spend time reflecting theologically on their situation in order to reach creative solutions about the overcoming of *han*. Different theological approaches remind us that we have to make a decision about the appropriate forms of reconciliation. One approach is a forward-looking Christian imperialism, which sweeps away the problem by forcibly imposing a vision of the Kingdom; the other needs to deal with the past, reaching deep into the wounds which need to be healed and looking for a new thing to emerge from the status of victim, the status of the oppressed. Liberation, then, emerges from the overcoming of *han* and new insights into reunification as a symbol and process of reconciliation.

Jubilee

One important theological concept which has been used in this context is that of Jubilee, which would allow church renewal, the church becoming a

---

1 'Declaration of the Churches in Korea on National Reunification and Peace' KNCC, 1988, quoted in Kim, op. cit., p. 167.

faith community for peace and reconciliation, and working together with all the churches, employing all the necessary means toward peace and reconciliation. The biblical concept of Jubilee as part of reconciliation, means allowing pardon, breathing space, and forgiveness into a neutral space where old grievances can be laid down, *han* expressed and separation to be overcome.

The theological reflection on war, on unjust structures of society, on hope and possibilities for understanding and healing Unreconciled communities shows us that in issues of separation and unity we must also look to non-western experiences and theologies to learn more about the Unreconciled among us and how to deal with their concerns. Such experiences and theology offer us new perspectives for change in our own situation and help us to consider those marks of mission which require us to transform unjust structures of societies everywhere and to tend with loving service those who have suffered.

Church unity

Finally, if we are considering the difficulties posed by the Unreconciled in our communities, and the questions of reconciliation between groups which are separated, we must also face the fact that the issue of church unity is just as critical a matter. Ecumenical working depends on first recognising the deep divisions which can exist between different Christians, whether those divisions relate to church tradition, to doctrine, or to moral and ecclesial issues. One can argue then that the mission of the Church, as it is variously understood by the denominations, should have a profoundly reconciliatory effect on ecumenical working, driving the need to overcome differences and mutual suspicions in favour of the greater good of telling the good news of Jesus Christ to others. Moreover, reconciliation doesn't just happen through ecumenical encounter; people have to keep working at it. Disagreement does not necessarily have to be overcome, but at the same time it cannot leave Christians in the same place. The journey to reconciliation is about living with that difference in such a way as to enrich the sharing of the gospel, not confusing its message or holding it back. As an ecumenical group, working on this book and other projects, MTAG members have been aware of the need to create unity out of diversity and our conversations, disagreements, differing denominational perspectives, and shared experience of prayer, worship and Christian faith all have been part of the mix for a fruitful and ongoing conversation.

Condemnation and Forgiveness

Neither do I condemn you. Go and do not sin again. (See John 7.53–8.11)

Within mission thinking and practice, reconciliation often gets confused with the issue of forgiveness. Forgiveness is a powerful theological concept which infuses all Christian relationships and sacraments. It is important that we weave into our understanding of mission that forgiveness is an integral part of the process. We do not, of course, have a monopoly on forgiveness, but there is something distinctively Christian about the way it is woven into our theology which sets it apart from the self-understanding of other religions and creates a particularly fruitful basis for testing inter-faith exploration and dialogue. Forgiveness is at the heart of the Lord's Prayer which Jesus gave us and a necessary requisite of Eucharistic liturgy. However, forgiveness can also be difficult, frightening and an obstacle to healing. We need to understand the relationship between reconciliation and forgiveness and why they are separate issues in mission. We can say that forgiving is that form of love which we extend to the 'enemy' without any pre-conditions. In forgiving the enemy we are not necessarily seeking to make him or her a friend. Pope John Paul II made this distinction very clear when he wrote, for the Day of Peace 2002 'The pillars of true peace are justice and that form of love which is forgiveness. Forgiveness is the opposite of resentment and revenge, not of justice.'[1] Robert Enright, the pioneer of forgiveness studies in the USA, focuses on letting go of resentment: 'Forgiveness is a willingness to abandon one's right to resentment, negative judgment, and indifferent behaviour toward one who unjustly injured us, while fostering the undeserved qualities of compassion, generosity, and even love toward him or her'.[2] Forgiveness then can have an important part to play in the rehabilitation of the Unreconciled, but it is not an automatic restorative, or panacea.

Reconciliation is what happens between self and Other or between different people or communities, forgiveness is what one does in one's own heart, either on an interior, personal level or as a corporate body. This means that while reconciliation will often entail or even require forgiveness, forgiveness may not end in reconciliation. Many Christians can feel hurt when they

---

1 Available at http://www.vatican.va/holy_father/john_paul_ii/messages/peace/documents/
   hf_jp-ii_mes_20011211_xxxv-world-day-for-peace_en.html.

2 Enright 1991, quoted in Robert D Enright, Suzanne Freedman and Julio Rique 'The
   psychology of interpersonal forgiveness' in Robert D Enright and Joanna North, *Exploring
   Forgiveness*, (Madison, Wisconsin: University of Wisconsin Press 1998) pp. 46–7.

have forgiven those who have injured them to discover that this does not automatically mend a relationship or restore the world to rightness. People can feel devastated when a relationship that they value has collapsed and find that forgiveness of adultery, unkindness or crime does not give them the restoration of love that they so desperately desire.

> I have forgiven my sister for the hurt she has caused my family, but now I don't know where she is or where she lives. I don't know her phone number or her email address. If only she would call and say 'I'm sorry. I've been a prat,' I would forgive her without question and invite her to stay with us as she used to do. But she is lost, and forgiving her and praying for her has not brought her home.

Fr Jim McManus explains:

> The aims of forgiveness and reconciliation are different. The goal of reconciliation is the restoration of friendship, of communion, of fellowship in the Spirit. The goal of forgiving is certainly to

prepare the way for reconciliation but its more immediate goal is the healing of one's own wounded heart. I think we can state it this way: the theological goal of forgiving is restoration of communion in the Spirit and the psychotherapeutic aim of forgiving is the healing of the broken heart.

Fr Jim points to the importance of recognising the damage to ourselves and the role which forgiveness plays in healing that damage. That is why the role of the one who is forgiving is also important, as either helping or hindering the process. Jesus indicates that forgiveness is not something which merely benefits the one who is forgiven. Forgiveness brings good to the forgiver, even if reconciliation cannot be achieved and carries a healing power from God. So forgiveness can be willed for its own sake by any hurt person. Moreover, we can argue that human beings have an absolute human right to forgive as a means to healing and restoration of their own selves. This is more helpful than talking about a moral obligation to forgive.

Forgiveness can also be the creative process in situations where reconciliation is impossible. For example, the one with whom we would like to be reconciled may be dead. That doesn't mean that we cannot forgive, even though in this life there will be no moment for making up. For some people it can help to write a letter or visit the grave. In these cases, prayer can provide a medium for forgiveness

Another situation in which forgiveness can be healing but reconciliation may not be appropriate is in situations where the one to be forgiven is an abuser. The forgiver may need to be protected and the abuser may need to know that forgiveness will not permit any situation where abuse might continue.

Further, if the person to be forgiven does not desire reconciliation and wants to be allowed to leave, then forgiveness may have to happen in the absence of reconciliation. Forgiveness cannot assume that all will be well because of the act of forgiving, but at the same time the fact that one person refuses to be reconciled does not nullify the forgiveness that is being offered. In this case the forgiver is exercising his or her right to forgive and thus lay down all feelings of hate, enmity and vengeance and by doing so heal their heart.

Forgiveness and justice

Many Christians believe that forgiveness wipes out the need for justice and lets those who have done hurt go free. This means that they retain their own personal pain until some form of justice is offered. But we can argue it is possible to separate these two things so that a person can say 'I forgive you from my heart and I will see you in court'. So a mother whose child has been hurt or damaged by another person can forgive in order to release herself from the cycle of pain and retributive feelings, but still pursue justice for her child, restitution, and perhaps also the making sure that other children cannot be so harmed in the future.

Stuart (solicitor)

I see a lot of people who are divorcing, who are making arrangements for children, making wills, etc. Although much of what I do sounds adversarial, negotiating with the 'other side' a lot of it is about reconciliation. With warring couples, we try to encourage mediation. When we get to court, we try to come to an agreement outside the courtroom – sometimes the experience of coming in front of a judge is enough to get people to sort things out. One of the things I do is to watch for signs for reconciliation – in my own clients and by negotiating with other solicitors involved. Reconciliation is always better. It's better for the kids, it's better for the opposed parties because it ends up being their decision, not a decision that's given to them from elsewhere and out of their hands. With people making wills and in dealing with probate, there's also sometimes a lot of reconciling that has to be done. The stuff I go through with people often brings difficult times and experiences to the surface and I try to suggest to people that they deal with it before they give me instructions. But of course, if they do give me instructions – well they're the client; they pay the bill. But when there is reconciliation, and things get settled quickly without escalation or further animosity, I feel like I might have helped a bit in helping them see clearer what they need to do.

The healing power of forgiveness to those who forgive is recognised by psychiatrists. The act itself is the therapeutic process. It does not seem to matter if those who are forgiven refuse to accept it or are unaware of it. The process of letting go of bitterness and resentment itself has therapeutic value and allows people to move away from being stuck in the memory and suffering attending dreadful deeds. Such people are provided with a means to climb out of the pit and move on. Even people who continue to be hated and despised by enemies, can reject that position and move towards wholeness. So when Jesus says 'love your enemies', and 'do good to those who persecute you' he is referring to the power of such an act to free people from the cycle of revenge by allowing benefit to flow in two directions. Refusing to hate back benefits those who respond with love, and benefits the enemies who are consumed with negative feelings and emotions. This creates the possibility for all concerned to grow and flourish in their spiritual journey and relationship to God. Forgiveness should be a proactive matter, not one which has to wait for some evidence of reconciliation.

Those who can't forgive

Is it right to forgive people who don't ask for forgiveness, who don't apologise or repent for the wrong they have done? Should we always demand repentance as the price of forgiveness? Repentance is an important measure of reconciliation in the New Testament, an act of will and heart to turn away from human evil and fasten the heart on God. The perpetrator of evil, whose heart remains hardened, cannot receive as a blessing the forgiveness that his victim may offer him.

But we must also take account of those people who cannot forgive and who remain in the land of the Unreconciled. We have to distinguish between the broken heart that feels it cannot forgive and the hardened heart that is determined not to forgive. The broken heart needs healing. We have to patiently open up to the broken heart the vision of the healing power of forgiveness and carefully explain the difference between forgiving and being reconciled. For example:

Susan

Susan is 46, married and the mother of 3 children. She lives in the Midlands and is a member of CSSA (Christian Survivors of Sexual Abuse). Current UK statistics suggest that 1 in 6 children are sexually abused before they reach the age of 16.

I was about eight years old when the abuse started. The friendly life guard at the swimming pool was an active paedophile. He molested my older brother, among others. Eventually he turned his attentions to me. My brother watched that first time, smiling at my bewilderment. The abiding memory is feeling so very, very small – the man could have picked me up and put me in his pocket.

Threats "not to tell" were left to my brother. Corrupted by this man, and mercilessly bullied at school, my brother started to molest me. I remained silent. My Christian faith kept the lid on my suffering. God's love to me was conditional on forgiveness, wasn't it?

My crisis began when my daughter approached her eighth birthday, and the horror of what happened to me finally dawned. I sought help through Christian literature, but it just told lovely stories about reconciliation. Trusted Christian friends offered well meaning advice, and in one case, an exorcism. The focus was praying for my abuser's redemption. It is not hard to see how in this context, forgiveness can allow abuse to thrive.

I allowed my brother supervised access to my children, but as his behaviour became more erratic, I chose to sever the relationship altogether. My husband and elderly parents wanted to know the reasons why. The truth was very hard to tell, and so I put myself to bed and stayed there.

I had some psychiatric treatment, but a feeling of guilt and low self-esteem remains. I would like to say 'The Lord's Prayer' and mean it – but I can't go as far as forgiveness. Truthfully, all I can do is try and understand what motivates behaviour, and not hold any hatred in my heart. I sometimes wonder how much more I could have achieved in life if the abuse had never happened. If the bud had not been blighted?

With permission of The Forgiveness Project: www.theforgivenessproject.com/stories/susan

Recent work in the Church of England[1] has pointed to the difficulty for some hurt people to approach the difficult matter of reconciliation and forgiveness within a church culture that expects them to put their hurt aside before they are ready. Expecting the person to fulfil the terms of the Lord's Prayer can add to their emotional burden, and the confession of sin can reinforce negative feelings of low self esteem and unworthiness. For some abused people, church is a place they feel they cannot deserve and which rubs in their isolation and alienation from the community by unwanted sharing and sometimes the unwanted physical contact of the Peace. Our Christian communities need to provide safe spaces for the hurt and the damaged, so that people can re-approach the language of love and reconciliation at their own pace and in their own time. In complex pastoral work of this kind, the Church in mission has to be very careful not to become part of the problem.

There is a difference however, between those who cannot forgive because of the need to work their pain and the hardened heart which is determined not to forgive at any cost. The person who is wedded to condemnation, perhaps using Christian teaching or Scripture as an excuse has a hardened heart that needs conversion. In such cases, we have to help those people to face what refusing forgiveness does to their own lives and well being and to consider the futility of trying to force the offender to repent or make up for the wrong that he or she has done. We have to invite those with hardened, or perhaps 'frozen' hearts to justify surrendering their God given right to forgive and help them to see that this only gives the offender more power over them. Giving up the tools of reconciliation only adds to the sum of human evil and in no way can begin the process of re-creation. If I refuse to forgive, I am also locked in the past. Refusal to forgive lies in a need to remain in control of the hurt and damage, but in fact means that the perpetrator and victim are locked together – and the perpetrator in fact retains control of the events which bind them.

---

1 See *Responding to Domestic Abuse: guidelines for those with pastoral responsibilities*, London: Church House Publishing 2006, available online at http://www.churchofengland.org/our-views/marriage,-family-and-sexuality-issues/domestic-abuse.aspx.

Forgiveness and forgetting

There is a prayer which comes from the concentration camp at Ravensbruck where 92,000 women and children died. This prayer, which is both glorious and challenging, was offered by a nameless woman and placed beside the dead body of a child. It helps us understand the miracle that we celebrate over Good Friday and Easter:

> O Lord, remember not only the men and women of good will, but also those of ill will. But do not remember all the suffering they have inflicted on us; remember the fruits we have bought, thanks to this suffering – our comradeship, our loyalty, our humility, our courage, our generosity, the greatness of heart which has grown out of all this, and when they come to the judgement let all the fruits that we have borne be their forgiveness.

©Marius Mézerette

Memory plays an important part in condemnation and forgiveness. In reconciliation, there is need to remember rightly. How this is done can pose a problem and is often embedded in those Jewish families who carry the burden of remembering and not forgetting the millions of their people and their particular relatives killed in the Holocaust. The past must not be subjected to whitewash, but equally, the pouring of energy into relentless pursuit of a particular form of justice, as in the Nazi hunters, raises the question of what is right use of human life and action in searching for justice. Beyond this, the need to remember in a helpful, positive way is true also for all whose past is blighted by atrocity. One woman whose sister was murdered, told the Forgiveness Project, movingly, that forgiveness means giving up all hope of a better past. So for her, forgiveness is not forgetting but remembering in a different way.[1] [2]

Memory binds both perpetrators and victims together. It is a link, often an unwanted or even unbearable link, that combines them. The insistence on sorting out the past can result in the creation of false or altered memories and a process of rewriting history to suit ourselves for better or worse. There have to be ways of processing memory that does not make the situation even more difficult. Forgiveness means putting those memories in context and creating something useful out of them, but that takes courage and effort as an unredeemed past can affect the present.

F

F was attacked in her home by a man who threatened her small children with a knife, stole from her and raped her. Talking about this experience later, she said that she was tormented by the thought that no matter what happened to this man, he could continue to remember her and repeat it in his imagination. Her humiliation and suffering and his power over and hatred for her, could potentially always be relived. For her, this meant that the rape was still present, if only in the man's memory. Time could pass, she could change and even move on, but the fact that memory can be recalled continued to torment her. 'If I could tear that memory out of his brain and erase it I would have some idea of it being *over*, but as long as he is alive, it is not over. It's there every day.'

This story shows that memory is very important. When those who are victimised suffer they must bear that memory of the event and such memories have the power to torment condemning the hurt person to an Unreconciled state. Reconciliation therefore means that there must be a mechanism for dealing with those memories. George Santayana famously said that if you cannot remember the past you are condemned to repeat it;[3] we must instead learn from our memories and release any poison that resides there. What a person needs is time, space and solidarity. It is repentance that makes a difference and can enables both victimisers and those who are victimised to get out of the repetitious cycle of mistakes.

We get a picture of this from the Beatitudes (Matthew 5.1–11; Luke 6.20–26) where there are three groups of people who are involved in God's desire for reconciliation. The first group are the victims, the poor and the

---

1 See: http://www.theforgivenessproject.com/stories/marian-partington.

2 *Don't Forgive Too Soon*, Paulist Press 1997, by Matthew Linn, Sheila Fabricant Linn and Dennis Linn, offers a five step programme for getting rid of the desire for vengeance but without passivity or giving up.

3 In *The Life of Reason*, volume 1 *Reason in Common Sense*, 1905–6.

mourners whose Unreconciled state is noticed by God and upon whom his love and grace must fall and with whom we must stand in solidarity. The second group are those who are involved in that reconciling work, the peacemakers, whose actions make that love and grace manifest. But there are also those referred to in the 'woe unto' sections of the Beatitudes in Luke whose damage and destruction hold back the Kingdom and whose behaviour must be addressed.

God's forgetting

In the Hebrew Scriptures there is a model for reconciliation through forgiveness in God's forgetting of the sins committed by Israel and remembering his love and future destiny for them. In this sense, it is important that we do not become trapped by memories which will prevent us moving towards God's intention for us and for the whole creation. This does not mean that God blanks or wipes out events in time, but rather the memory of the past does not affect the intention or purpose of the *missio dei*. In the New Testament we find an even more powerful example of this process in the meeting between the Risen Lord and Peter, where Jesus restores to Peter his guilty past, wiping out his threefold denial by asking him three times if he loves him. Jesus does not do this to condemn him but to make that forgiven past the foundation for a new and extended identity as Jesus' disciple (John 21.15–19). God remembers sins, but forgets them when they have been named as iniquities and forgiven (Isaiah 43.18–19; 25; cf 65.17; see also Jeremiah 31.34). The memory of sin must be kept alive for a while, so that it can provide the material for repentance and transformation to occur. But then it must be let die so that a new relationship can be formed. The memory of offence, sustained beyond repentance, clouds both the memory of past love and the vision of future reconciliation. So in God's purposes reconciliation and forgiveness are not the same. Reconciliation among people and communities may not involve actual forgiveness (yet).

What, therefore, does it mean to say that the truth (ie the truth in Jesus) will set us free (John 8.32)? Suffering may take place but there is no clear focus for its origin. For example:

> I was adopted. I loved my adoptive parents but there came a time when I had to look for truth and understanding about how and why I was adopted. But what I found out didn't help me make sense of what happened. There was undoubtedly pain at the heart of the adoption decision, but unlike a clear abuse, I didn't have a mechanism to deal with it. The 'truth' in my case did not offer a clear evil or a given perpetrator.

A similar situation can occur on a much larger scale because we live in a world where opposing powers can wage war talking about doing 'the right thing', or pursuing a 'war on terror' or 'jihad' and using God-language to back up their decisions, yet the result is quite simply the slaughter of people they don't know. Civilians caught up in such a war then die in despair and even if they want to forgive, *who* can they forgive? They are condemned to be Unreconciled because the focus for a path to reconciliation is unclear. Peace-making or effecting a ceasefire or even a surrender, is not enough. The perpetrators are people the Unreconciled don't know unless they are described by some general name like 'America' or 'the West' or 'Al-Quaeda' or 'The Taliban'. This is why solidarity with our neighbours is so important. When we look at the way war is waged in today's world, we see the name of God is often profaned. We need to find out, as a mission task, how to purify and hallow the name of God of this profane use, otherwise the words 'Hallowed be thy Name' in the Lord's Prayer just sound empty. Reconciliation and mission require that we know our neighbours, whether they be friends or enemies. But is it part of our makeup and part of the process that leads to reconciliation, that we need someone to blame?

Blame

The need to place blame exists deep in the human psyche. It is even more prevalent in the litigious western world. In our society accidents never happen, there is always someone out there to be responsible, who must take blame and who must repay.

> A young man fell under a train and was killed. It was not clear whether he fell, jumped or was pushed. He had been drinking but not much. Counselling his grieving friends, it was very clear that they need a focus of blame for their anger and misery and to give meaning to nameless fear. Somebody or something must be responsible or accountable for their grief, even (or especially) God. For his friends, looking at mere contingency or pure accident meant looking into the void. Even if the coroner decided it was an accident, his friends were determined that something must have 'killed' him.

Our deep need to place blame (and absolve oneselves from blame) focuses the need for human redemption and an understanding of grace. But there are problems with the outworkings of this. What happens if you get a cycle of behaviour in which people are told what to do and punished if they don't accept responsibility for those actions? In some places people are now being penalised for being obese or for smoking by not being referred for treatment. They are not forgiven if they don't repent. What lies at the back of this? Do we genuinely care about people's health or secretly want to see people punished because they have been enjoying themselves, eating, smoking or enjoying sex? Does this idea then create resentment that taxpayers' money is then spent on restoring over-indulgers to health? Blame can be an excuse for cheap understanding, where we are too lazy to look into the underlying causes and the stories of people's lives.

As we saw in the chapter on Otherness and Self, Israel Selvanayagam directs our attention to a well known bible story which is often overlooked in terms of its potential to look at blame and forgiveness: the story of Jacob and Esau in the Hebrew Scriptures (Genesis 33:1–11). Jacob is cunning and wily and able to turn crisis situations to his advantage, leading to Esau giving him his birthright. Further, Jacob, helped by his mother, steals his father's blessing by pretending to be Esau. Esau is furious and wants to kill Jacob. He is filled with the need to blame Jacob and harbour a grudge against him. Yet twenty years later when Jacob and Esau meet again, the expectation that Esau's need to blame and seek revenge will have smouldered away for the intervening period until it ignites at the face of Jacob is countered by a very different picture:

Jacob's meeting of his brother Esau after twenty years is very dramatic. It starts with the effect of a bitter past. "Jacob looked up and there was Esau coming with four hundred men. He divided the children between Leah and Rachel and the two slave-girls. He put the slave girls and their children in front, Leah with her children next, and Rachel and Joseph in the rear. He himself went on ahead of them, bowing low to the ground seven times as he approached his brother" (33:1–3). This shows his precautions and strategy to avert any possible avengement. But what happened was something he never expected. "Esau ran to meet him and embraced him; he threw arms round him and kissed him, and they both wept" (33:4). Introduction of the contingent and greetings followed. It is not just a reconciliation between two individuals but also acceptance of what they have become and acquired over the years. Esau was impulsively overtaken by the joy of reunion with his brother. No mention of the past in the context of wholehearted forgiveness. It is like God's forgiveness as it is reflected in the words, 'I remember your sins no more' (Isaiah 43.25).[1]

The story presumes that Jacob's actions are hanging over him waiting for retribution and this expectation comes to a climax in the wrestling match with a mysterious stranger in the night (Genesis 32.24ff). However the cycle of blame and retribution stops when Esau embraces his brother in a way reminiscent of the story of the prodigal. In embracing Esau, Jacob embraces liberation and the chance to be free once more.

Christian accounts of the atonement tell us that the cross offers the chance to blame Jesus. God does not retaliate but absorbs the blame and stops the cycle. What the advertisements for stopping smoking and changing lifestyle don't offer, but the Gospels do, is that a changed person brings *joy*. When a person returns from the state of being Unreconciled and reconciliation is made truly possible, this creates joy in those who have longed for the reconciliation. So we too should celebrate repentance as the Father does at the return of the prodigal. One person's repentance creates rejoicing in

---

1 Israel Selvanayagam, op.cit.

heaven, and earth should reflect the life of heaven. It is a capacity in all of us, enabled by God's grace, to rejoice for those who have repented, and the repentant person should be assured of that joy in the creation and the people around. Even within the Church, we are not good at rejoicing and celebrating those who repent nor when we are released from the cycle of blame. But if, as churches, we refuse to enjoy that foretaste in our community by concentrating on punishment, expect to enter that joy later on?

Confession and Penitence

We have already seen that incomplete mechanisms for confession can block the road both to reconciliation and to the growth and emergence of something new. Our society can make it difficult to accept responsibility and say sorry. For example, in 2004, body parts were taken from dead children at Alder Hey hospital and stored without consent. Despite the distress and pain of the parents when these actions came to light, there were legal reasons for not saying sorry straightaway. [1] Conversely, sentencing and parole in prisons can be affected by how much remorse people show. It matters whether you are sorry or not. But for some perpetrators admission of guilt and expression

1 See the account of the reconciling work of the burial service for the unidentified babies at
  http://www.guardian.co.uk/uk/2004/aug/06/health.alderhey

of remorse is far away from the present moment of trial and conviction. The processes of law do not facilitate this means of reconciliation to unfold from the beginning.

Within the Church, we are capable of forgetting to provide sufficient means of sacramental confession (the sacrament of reconciliation) to allow our human fault to be released into the ambit of God's forgiveness and our own. So, paradoxically, perpetrators of sin can remain victims of their own sin, unless provided with some means of telling their story. The Church needs to provide, as part of its own mission, sacred spaces and times during which the truth can be named and explored. Finding creative ways to allow people to lay down such burdens is a mission imperative. Repentance needs grace and looks to a bigger justice than we have to offer. Our eschatological hope is that 'I will know as I am fully known'. Only God really knows, the rest has to be taken on trust.

Fear and Shame

Another matter which we need to address and from which Christians in the west need urgently to listen to Christians in the developing world, is the matter of intellectualisation of concepts such as reconciliation and forgiveness. We often have problems with theologies of embodiment, so we don't consider what such concepts mean in terms of humanity and intimacy. Yet we all know that to be unreconciled to another person can result in refusal to touch. The loss of human intimacy is a mark of estrangement. Because of this, we do not have a particularly developed concept of shame.

In the Indian world, however, there is a powerful concept of shame. People need to be responsible; the last straw is to feel shame, just as in the creation stories Adam and Eve were ashamed of their nakedness when their eyes were opened after the Fall. Conversely, losing the stigma of shame creates a path to salvation, but if a person is incapable of feeling shame, then they have lost their humanity. As Christians, we should talk about our fear and shame.

Despite this, we use underlying and often unspoken concepts of fear and shame to control people. We see this in the history of gender relations. A double standard in sexual relations has meant that men are beyond shame, but shame has often controlled women's lives. Repentance can mean you must accept who you really are in both dark and light. God roots out the way we can cause pain to others and allows this acceptance. What will it be like to stand in the presence of light and love? In Orthodox theology, heaven and hell both experience the divine light.

In one part of Africa, people who have offended the community are named and shamed, but the process involves a ritual in which the offenders accompany the village community to a river where they are washed in the blood of a dog. This is the worst thing that could happen to them. Then they are washed clean and are deemed to have washed all their guilt away

with the pollution. The offence enters the blood and is washed away. It is utterly gone and they are forgiven. They are then accompanied back to the village amid rejoicing.

For us, baptism and communion involve reference to the death of a criminal and it becomes the means of ritual cleansing. Our hope is enshrined in someone who was executed as a criminal, one perceived as a danger to society. That death becomes a powerful act offering recovery; eternal good emerges from the cursing and the shameful death. In the sacraments naming and shaming in fact identifies us with Christ and releases us into his freedom. We should think more clearly about the atonement idea: to bring a thing to justice, someone must die as a scapegoat.

In India this has been raised by a Hindu scholar, wanting to know how washing in the blood of Christ means purification. As a vegetarian he has an antipathy to blood. How do we explain our language, that by 'blood of Christ' we mean 'pain of God' or 'God's suffering love'. This makes sense, but we do not bother to explain it to others. The cross too is God's suffering and 'blood' is the language of that suffering. Jesus said that unless we eat his flesh and blood we will not have life. But what does that mean? In western culture, this concept sounds disgusting, but in India the idea of closeness to flesh and blood means intimacy. So when Jesus says these things, who is being addressed? The poor can understand Jesus' language, but not the Jewish elite. In tribal societies, blood means relationship. In marriage, the symbol is not tying the knot but one of blood and flesh. This is what Jesus meant.

We should also address the concept of 'fear' because in our typical Christian language we don't talk about fear and shame. In Revelation, the angel flying with the eternal gospel (14.7) says 'fear God'. So the foundation of the eternal gospel is fear/reverence/profound respect for God. All other things are superstructures erected on this. Muslims also affirm this – you should pay homage to God alone. This is not the same as being afraid of God or being frightened by God, but of accepting responsibility before God. So recovery of the proper use of the idea of fearing God can lay foundations for reconciliation and Christian mission.

Hell and Heaven

Towards a theology of the Unreconciled

Why bother?

We have seen that Christian mission means seriously to address those groups of Unreconciled in our societies who are in need of help to find the power and will to move towards some sort of reconciliation. We have also learned that exploring such issues reveals more to us of our own place among the Unreconciled, and shows us the hidden parts of our unreconciled nature. However, why bother? Unless we have some kind of expectation of some purpose and meaning to the reconciling process, then all we are doing is tinkering with the way things are, making ourselves feel a bit better, absolving the questions we cannot answer by investing in doing 'good'.

The Christian creed which is recited in churches says 'we look for the resurrection of the dead and the life of the world to come', but what does this really mean? Heaven, or the life of the world to come, is a concept which requires a picture of the ultimately Reconciled. What does this mean? What does heaven look like? One place we can start is back with the Bible's account of how things are meant by God to be. The creation stories in Genesis paint a picture for us of a created world in which God is eternally present, for God walks in the Garden of Eden and interacts freely with human beings. The creation is blessed by God who delights in it, and pronounces it 'good'; it is intrinsically good in itself. At the heart of this goodness are the creatures who are made in the image of God, living in the light of his love and his blessing. But the story seeks to explain how the universe we experience is not at all like this image of perfection, peace and harmony. Because of Adam and Eve's disobedience, turning away from sharing God's vision and trying to impose their own way on the world, time begins to unravel and the world as we now know it comes into being. After the expulsion from the Garden, Adam and Eve's world becomes our world, recognisable from the work and effort they have to put in to make a living and build a life. Life is tough and soon becomes full of murder, mayhem and misery. This is the country of the Unreconciled, familiar territory – so what do we have to do to get back to the world as God wants it?

The answer is that we cannot go back. Human beings exist in unfolding time stretching onward towards an unknown future. As time continues we come to know the messy reality of human existence and so must work to create order and society. Peace and harmony are no longer the natural order of affairs, even though the memory of that primordial intention never

quite leaves us. Adam and Eve must mend the clothes God gives them and cultivate the ground for food (Genesis 3.17; 21). As the earth evolves and time continues, human beings must work towards a way of living which is fuelled by the promise of the creation story, a condition of existence in which people co-exist with God in the creation and disorder is no more. But we can't reverse any of this. There is no retracing our steps to the angel with the flaming sword. We cannot unmake history, or forget our past. But then we discover, that as human beings made in the image of God, and prompted by God's call, we have within us the seeds of creative possibility, we can learn, make, do, strive, heal, change. The creation stories too tell us more about our place in the disordered world. The world of human experience is full of danger, disaster and brokenness. Much of this is due to the exercise of human will and far from God's intention for human beings stated in Genesis, that the created order be under the stewardship and care of human beings, as co-creators and partners with God. Scripture offers many stories of both creation and destruction in human experience and it is notable that human beings' relation to the destructive experiences is mapped out in terms of their relation to God. The cataclysmic destruction of the Flood is detailed against a call from God to save, to resist the destruction and rebuild what is broken and ruined. The end of this story is a covenant between human beings and God, underlining God's saving intent and reaffirming the need to work towards healing and saving in human life (Genesis 9.1–17). Our task then, is to know, intimately, the condition of the Unreconciled, and to find out from God what we can do to change it.

We are all heaven-makers

What does all this teach us about the process of reconciliation in the world of the Unreconciled? It is that reconciliation in all its forms makes the vision of heaven a little more clear. It has an eschatological emphasis and brings with it a more emphatic statement of the hope that is contained in the final lines of the creed. No acts of reconciliation in human experience are final or complete; they are foreshadows of the new thing which is promised when God remakes all that is and establishes the new creation. It is a task for human beings to assist in that process. So the churches in mission are heaven-makers, and the end of that mission is achieved beyond our human lives. The philosopher Nicholas Woltersdorff, whose son Eric was killed in a mountaineering accident, writes that reconciliation for him can never be complete until he is reunited with his dead son, and that this reconciling, reuniting act will itself announce the reality of heaven: 'when I say my first words to Eric, then God's reign will be here.'[1] The grief of bereavement then, commits us to the world of the Unreconciled, but we are reminded through the funeral service that God desires that suffering and separation

---

1 Nicholas Woltersdorff, op.cit., p. 78.

should be overcome by his love and that reconciliation awaits us if we align our will with his. It is perhaps not surprising then that dying people often report a sense of separation being overcome as they die and believe they can see or hear other loved ones who have died, at the edge of consciousness. Whatever these experiences mean, a good death can entail a sense of rejoining or restoring lost relationships of which the ultimate such restoration is return to God. Such threshold experiences should recall us to the heart of our belief: 'we look for the resurrection of the dead and the life of the world to come'. This comes across strongly in the resurrection appearances where Jesus returns to his disciples and offers them incontrovertible evidence, not just of life after death, but of continued relationship with others and with God: 'go to my brothers and say to them, 'I am ascending to my Father and your Father, to my God and your God' (John 20.17).

In the medieval dream-vision known as *Pearl,* a father, grieving for his dead infant daughter, meets her adult form in a dream and is told that reconciliation will reunite them beyond the grave, but for now he is to live his life in renewed understanding that the vision of that heavenly meeting will now transfigure his life forever. He must spend his time working towards that moment in sure faith and try to offer that vision to everyone. The visionary language of this story, with its images of brilliant shining and glory which increase as the story progresses, suggests to readers that reconciliation brings with it an ability to see beyond the mundane and speak the hope of the life to come into any dark place.

What does hell teach us?
The other side of the reconciling work that foreshadows heaven is a picture of those people who remain eternally Unreconciled. Those human beings who cannot or will not respond to what is life-giving and life-affirming find themselves separated from God, the condition of hell.

Thereby Cocytus wholly was congealed.
With six eyes did he weep, and down three chins
Trickled the tear-drops and the bloody drivel.

At every mouth he with his teeth was crunching
A sinner, in the manner of a brake,
So that he three of them tormented thus.

To him in front the biting was as naught
Unto the clawing, for sometimes the spine
Utterly stripped of all the skin remained.

This passage from Dante's *Divine Comedy,* marks the point at which Dante has reached the very depths of hell among the traitors.[1] Here is Judas Iscariot, in Dante's time the worst of all traitors for having betrayed Jesus,

---

1 *The Inferno*, Canto XXXIV

welded in misery and torment to Lucifer, being chewed and having his skin clawed off.

Christians down the ages have been pursued by the power of these images, with the echoes of tortured souls wailing in despair, and all the imaginative agonies of Hieronymus Bosch to remind us to stick to the narrow path. The entrance to Hell, Dante tells us, reads *Abandon hope all ye who enter here.* As a place for the ultimately Unreconciled, there is only eternity without progression, nothing new, surprising or liberating can ever happen again. This is something that Jesus tells us in a number of admonitory sayings. While God has given us lives to lead, we can make decisions and orient our wills to God's purpose for us. For as long as we do that, there is no closure on the Unreconciled state. If we shut down all those possibilities and define our lives purely by selfishness, evil acts and refusal to look for God's desire for us, we are likely to get stuck like that and so find it impossible to 'look…for the life to come'. This is the force of the story Jesus tells of the rich man and Lazarus (Luke 16.19ff).

As an eschatological idea, some theologians[1] hope or believe that in the end every self-reflective creature may be reconciled to God in the face of a love that never gives up. The creed makes this clear in the statement of belief that says that Christ descended into hell before being reunited with the Father in heaven. The harrowing of hell, as part of Christ's own mission, is an understanding often overlooked in Christian tradition, in which God's saving love through Christ, breaks into the place of separation and offers the

1 For example, Jacques Maritain, Hans Urs von Balthasar, Karl Rahner. Also see the Doctrine Commission of the Church of England's *The Mystery of Salvation* Church House Publishing, 1995.

gift of life to those waiting for reconciliation with God. In fact, concepts of hell developed from the idea of two realms of the dead. 'Sheol', before the resurrection, was a place where people were waiting to be set free as in the poem quoted below, but there was also another place where people could be separated from God for ever. But in the tradition of the harrowing of hell, the idea remains that God never gives up on us and will send his Son to save us from the Unreconciled state – if we will accept his love for us in the end. So in the traditional iconography of the harrowing of hell, Jesus leads the lost from the lion's mouth, holding their hands, while the Devil lies bound beneath his feet and usually looking very grumpy.

But this iconography also has a birthing idea within it. The souls are sometimes depicted as emerging from the body of the hell-creature, small and naked. Jesus is the midwife, giving them a helping hand and receiving them gently into their new existence with him, in his world, bring hope and light into despair and darkness.[1] In the theology of St Ephrem the Syrian from the fourth century, Sheol, the realm of the dead, is the last womb from which Jesus himself emerges, leading his people into resurrection life. In one of his Nisibene Hymns, Death says:

I will haste and close the gates of Sheol before this Dead One
Whose death has spoiled me.
Whoever hears will wonder at my humiliation
That by a Dead Man who is without I am overcome.
All the dead seek to go forth, but this one presses to enter in.
A medicine of life has entered into Sheol and has restored life to its dead.
Who then has brought in and hidden from me that living fire
Which has loosed the cold and dark womb of Sheol?
Nisibene Hymns 36.14[2]

Therefore reconciliation is a powerful process for change, transformation and the establishing of that which is good. To use our birth analogy, the harrowing of hell is a bringing to birth of what has been suffering in long labour, there is midwifery and love's work is done: 'we know that the whole creation has been groaning in labour pains until now; and not only the creation, but we ourselves, who have the first fruits of the Spirit, groan inwardly while we wait for adoption, the redemption of our bodies. For in hope we were saved' (Romans 8.22–24). Similarly, in the book of Revelation (Apocalypse), the vision of the establishment of God's reign is filled with birth metaphors (eg Revelation 12.1–6) and delivery from a place of evil and stagnation (eg Revelation 18.4). By means of the Lord's saving midwifery, the Edenic state of the Reconciled is restored:

---

1 See Sheila Cassidy (1994) *Light from the Dark Valley: Reflections on Suffering and the Care of the Dying* (Notre dame, Indiana: Ave Maria Press) pp. 60–1.

2 Quoted in Thomas Buchan (2004) *"Blessed is he who has brought Adam from Sheol": Christ's descent to the dead in the theology of St Ephrem the Syrian* (Piscataway, NJ: Gorgia's Press).

See the home of God is among mortals.
He will dwell with them as their God;
They will be his peoples,
And God himself will be with them;
He will wipe every tear from their eyes.
Death will be no more;
Mourning and crying and pain will be no more,
For the first things have passed away' (Revelation 21.3–4).

Releasing people from hell on earth

Hell of course, does not just mean what happens to us after death. Hell is a place which any person can inhabit if their life on earth is marked by disease, poverty, tragedy or other suffering. Hell has traditionally been offered to people as images of destruction without help of reparation as we have seen, but Hell is also a condition of breakdown, offered in images of burning destruction, pain, fear, misery and eternal suffering and many people know what it is like on a daily basis. Reconciliation then, as part of mission, must be committed to social justice and the ending of hell for people. We cannot imagine or work towards heaven until we put paid to the hell where others reside.

'Purgatory' and reconciliation

It is interesting that in some recent books and TV series there has been an exploration of the world of the dead that exist neither in this life nor the next. In these series, the characters inhabit a particular kind of Unreconciled world, prevented from moving on by their ties to the world, their issues or their unresolved circumstances. For example the TV series Ashes to Ashes and Lost both came to their conclusions in 2010. In Ashes to Ashes, it turned out that the police station manned by DCI Hunt was in fact Hunt's own invention. Killed as young police officer fancying himself Gary Cooper in High Noon, the world he invents stars himself as the gung-ho, fast driving, gun-slinging all action hero. Into this world he takes other murdered police officers, helping them work out their unfilled ambitions, dreams and needs as they help others and rid Gene's fantasy world of bad people. In the final series of Ashes to Ashes, the devil comes into this world, trying to discredit Gene's work and recruit his lost souls for his infernal domain. Seduced by promises of money, easy work and pretty girls, horrified and angry after finding out how their lives were cut short, they stop on the brink, but in the end love and loyalty drive them back to Gene and at last to a new life as they leave him and enter not the pearly gates but the pub, with Winston, the publican, as an unusual St Peter. Similarly, in the final episode of Lost, the people discover that they are not survivors of the plane crash but dead people who have created a new world out of their experiences in order to work out their remaining issues. Their lives on the island and their lives revealed in their back stories have to be reconciled, wrongs righted, restraints lifted, sins repented and relationships mended. Similarly, in Alice Sebold's *The Lovely Bones* (released as a film in 2010) a murdered girl creates an afterlife around her as she remains bound to the life she left, her family and the person who murdered her.[1]

These explorations posit the idea of a Purgatory in which people who die in an Unreconciled state have the opportunity to fit themselves for heaven before moving on to that ultimate reconciliation.

Christian traditions vary widely on the question of whether any kind of Purgatory actually exists, what such a state entails, whether it's a bit like Sheol (see above) and whether living Christians can do anything to affect the existence of people who may be there. We have argued for a different way at looking at these issues, with the suggestion that we are all in some way Unreconciled and that final state of becoming who we are meant to be is in God's hands in God's eternity. What is clear, is there is an interest in this whole area in popular culture around us provoking comment and discussion on what it means to have unresolved issues and unfulfilled lives. We need to engage with this culture and share our faith as a way of understanding and dealing with these issues.

Judgement

Another important theological idea in which lies between the world of the Unreconciled and an eschatological reconciliation, is that of judgement. It is sometimes offered in ancient religious traditions in the old Egyptian sense of a weighing of souls against a feather. If your sins weigh you down, you will not be offered heaven. In other religions, the path to heaven or hell is a bridge or tightrope over a fire or chasm and you are pulled in one direction or another by your sins or deeds. But the entire concept of judgement is more complex than this either/or picture and does more things in our psyche. It meets a deep spiritual and psychological need to account for our humanity and human life, its purpose, worth and value, no matter how long or short that life proves to be. Further, that account of who and what we are requires serious attention and reconciling action on behalf of the one who judges. Without judgement, we will remain unreconciled to our human experience. In Julian Barnes' novel *A History of the World in 10½ chapters*, the man who asks to be judged is outraged to be told only 'You're ok'.[2] Surely a human life requires more attention, more notice?

How does the Unreconciled life meet the divine life?

The concept of judgement also requires us to think about how God receives our unreconciled human experience and adds it to the divine life. Consequently, reconciliation does not mean trying to recreate the Edenic

---

1 These films, TV series and books are included for study as downloadable resources with synopses, and questions for discussion in the 'Dream' section of www.spiritualjourneys. org.uk.

2 Julian Barnes, (1989), *A History of the World in 10 ½ Chapters*, (London: Jonathan Cape).

experience at the end of time, experience replaced by a return to innocence or some sort of cosmic forgetting. In Revelation, the woundedness of Christ is not cancelled out or wiped clean, but exists in eternity. Rather it is about the experiences of self-reflective creatures adding into the eternal love of God, folding the creation back into God's own self. We know that this happens because of the Ascension, where Jesus is taken into heaven complete with his story of Incarnation and with his experience of human life and death. The idea of intercession, similarly, carries within it the sense of the transcription of human experience into the divine world. When we pray, we tell God what it is like to be us and heaven is enriched by the experience of the saints. Scripture and tradition repeat this idea in other stories, where people are caught up into heaven intact and God assumes their life and experience. The story of Elijah and the tradition of the Assumption of the Virgin Mary are two examples of such narratives.

In Jostein Gaarder's story, *Through a Glass Darkly*, a young girl dying of cancer is assured by an angel that God wants to know all the experiences of her short life, because they are precious to Him and he is waiting to hear everything of her living, loving and dying.[1] In Rosemary Kay's book *Saul*, the tragically short life of her baby, born at 23 weeks, is re-presented as an account of an extraordinary life, recounted by Saul himself, as he struggles with the impossibility of doing 'This Living' in a body that is barely formed and not mature enough to survive and which is given up in the end to a larger and more wonderful reality that his short life makes sense of.[2] Reconciliation, then, prepares us for the act of judgement, the bringing before God of everything that we have experienced, felt and known, the totality of that life. For Christians, Jesus' death on the cross and his resurrection tells us all we need to know about how God had made it possible for the Unreconciled to enter a final reconciliation.

We perhaps see this most powerfully in the parable of the Prodigal (Luke 15). The son leaves the Father and plunges into the heart of an Unreconciled life, forgetting his origin and purpose, squandering his gifts and resources. The turning point comes when he recognises his condition and knows who and what he has become. From this point of self-recognition he can begin to think about reconciliation – what he has to do and say to achieve forgiveness: 'Father, I am not worthy to be called your son'. The parable leads us from the Father's house to the world of the Unreconciled and then winds back to the place of reconciliation, where the Father receives with joy the returned Son, ruined by excess, unclean from contact with the pigs, abject and hopeless, and takes all that experience back into the household, restoring him to all that he was meant to be. Things are not the same as they were before; no one is pretending that the inheritance hasn't been squandered, but the reconciliation of Father and Son brings joy beyond measure.

---

1 Jostein Gaarder, (1998), *Through a Glass Darkly*, (London: Orion).
2 Rosemary Kay, (2000) *Saul*, (New York: St Martin's Press).

Kingdom

How then do we translate the reconciling work we attempt to do among the Unreconciled on earth, into the vision of heaven that is beyond our lifetime and human existence? Jesus offers us the vision of Kingdom as the means to that translation. The Kingdom is both that which is already among us and a future we can work towards. It has both present and future states. Jesus points us again and again to the Unreconciled among us whose lives must be transformed: the poor, the outcast, the physically sick and the mentally ill, those in prison, the debtors, and those ruined by human weakness and evil. Reconciliation is both a sign of the kingdom and one of the processes which establishes the kingdom. 'Go back and report to John what you hear and see: The blind receive sight, the lame walk, those who have leprosy are cured, the deaf hear, the dead are raised, and the good news is preached to the poor'. (Matthew 11.4–5) To this end this transformation in the lives of the Unreconciled is a powerful generator of mission. More to the point, mission does not really exist unless it is powered by reconciliation.

'The will to reconciliation may begin as of a desire to end hostilities or make the neighbourhood safer, and as such it is enormously important and beneficial. The task of the Christian, however, is to extend the process inwards into the hearts of men and women were it ceases to be 'mere business' and becomes an exercise in bringing about the Kingdom of God.'[1]

Time

Because of the double notion of Christ's kingdom, we have to realise that our timeframes for understanding and responding to the Unreconciled are different from those experienced by most people in our western society. Our culture needs things to happen 'now' so that things are clear, principled or all sewn up. But Christians have been 'given time' so we can allow for more mess, not structure, because these things are not all up to us and can work themselves out in God's economy. Consequently the Christian missionary notion would be that in any situation it is never 'too late' for reconciliation to take place. There is no equivalent mission action of the solicitor who decides that the time for reconciliation is past or the politician who says the deadline for a ceasefire or surrender is now over. God is prepared to wait forever for the Unreconciled and in nurturing his seed, we have to be prepared for long incubation, if that's what it takes. But the other side of this requirement in mission to learn how to wait, how to endure with patience, is the need to discern when God's propitious time actually comes. Many Christians, on fire for God's mission, have problems with this kind of discernment, and may forge ahead with brilliant ideas and initiatives, without having checked out the situation or prepared the ground. Premature birth of reconciling work carries the same problems; – the results may be not fully

---

1 Gabriel Daly (1998) 'Forgiveness and Community' in Alan Falconer (ed) *Reconciling Memories* (Dublin: Columba Press)

formed and may not survive the rigours of exposure. Determining the right time for reconciling mission is a skill that needs to be worked at in every Christian church and in every Christian life.

For example, Canon Andrew White, writing to the Mission Theological Advisory Group about the difficulties of making progress in places like Iran, Palestine and Iraq reminds us that we may need to invest huge amounts of patient waiting in the peace process, something that governments find unsustainable and so is always crippled by lack of funds. He says:

> 'The starting point is often beginning with enabling each side to hear the other's story. Just to come to this point can in itself take many months or even years... As the encounter happens there is often a huge surprise at the pain that is experienced by each side in the conflict. It often takes months or even years to get people to engage with each other. The interim work is often just getting to know the issues. Listening to their stories in the ways that they wish to express them.'

One of the reasons for this is that most processes of reconciliation have a turning point which people may not be not prepared for. There is no algorithm for grace. Eschatological hope, that beautiful vision that *Pearl* holds out to the grieving father, is needed because often people stuck in intractable positions feel that reconciliation cannot be achieved. The turning point is often a surprise which suddenly changes everything and allows something new and unexpected to emerge. But there can also be a turning point in another direction when we need to be ready for urgent and immediate action as a church or mosque is blown up or violence breaks out suddenly and catastrophically and the world of the Unreconciled seems suddenly to take an even stronger grip.

Heavenly Peace

Hell, the place where the Unreconciled must languish, is for so many people the experience of being caught up in appalling conflict. Peace-making, then, as a reconciling work, is much more than achieving the cessation of hostilities. What reconciliation needs to do as more than just keeping the peace is address the trauma of the war experience for those who have endured it. Reconciliation must deliver people such as child soldiers from the loss of their childhood, and help those whose lives have been defined by killing to discover new possibilities for human existence. Reconciling action also requires economic restoration and political stability, the freedom to think and decide. Yet so many enforced attempts to bring such reconciliation, as so painfully evidenced by the war in Iraq, result only in more images of hell on earth – suicide bombings, mass murder, deprivation and fear. It is not enough simply to deplore the war in Iraq, or to lament the horror of 9/11 and 7/7 in western countries, although prophetic lament may be entirely part of our response. Although George Bush argued that God desires that we pursue a war against terror, God's reconciling work must penetrate to the heart of the terrorist and call that person neighbour, brother, sister. There is no doubt that this is a tremendously difficult task, which defies easy words and the rhetoric of peace-making. When the Twin Towers fell, the first thing to rise from Ground zero was the Cross, made of twisted, burned and tortured metal. This symbolic action defies easy words, but what it did represent, clearly, was the memory of God's saving work in a place of ruin, disorder and death and a reminder of the job of human beings to be inspired by God's work in Christ and bring about peace, reconciliation and a new creation in that place.

Perhaps the clearest reminders that we have today of those Unreconciled who live in a hell we have made, are those people caught up and ruined by war. Reconciliation for Christians is not just a matter of peacemaking but of helping those who are maimed and injured in body, mind and spirit, and bringing to birth a vision of a world in which such damage and injury would not just be kept at bay, but become unthinkable.

More Hell on Earth
In any theology of the Unreconciled, one other contemporary issue occupies every part of the news media. We live in a time when the damage we have done to our planet demands our attention. If we are all the Unreconciled, through our disobedience to God, then one of the ways in which that disobedience is most marked is in our refusal to respond to God's desire for us to undertake responsible and caring stewardship of the planet on which we live and of the other living things that surround us. It is not surprising then, that the fifth and perhaps most neglected mark of mission is that of respecting the integrity of creation and renewing the life of the earth. Yet this is powerful reconciling work. The Edenic vision and the heavenly vision require us to appreciate the planet and the diversity of its life, to respect that life and to work to undo the harmful effects of human behaviour on the ecology of the planet and the multiple environments in which creatures live. So currently, warnings about the damage we have already done to the environment paint a picture of the hell on earth that we can create if we do not try to deliver a renewed creation. There will be desert where once green things grew; we will lose so many animals and plants which once graced our world; we will not have the fuels and resources we need to prosper.

Reconciliation for mission in terms of the environment requires a particular kind of birth. In the first place it must change the perceived view that Christians believe that human beings dominate the earth and are more important than other living things. Rather we must realise that we are the Unreconciled in relation to the ecological balance of the planet. Reconciliation demands that we investigate what it means to be stewards of the creation and build that into our mission understanding. Destruction of

habitats and the extinction of living things are proper cause for prophetic lament. Trying to undo the damage and create new environments for living things is reconciling work in the spirit of the Ark. Mission through environmental action brings to birth a scriptural assertion: the Earth is the Lord's and all that is in it (psalm 24.1). However, Christians are now responding to the challenge of the mess and disorder brought about by squandering the earth's resources.

A Rocha UK[1]

A Rocha UK is a movement of people – staff, volunteers and Friends; working together for the good of God's creation. Our work across the UK includes practical conservation initiatives and environmental education, both of which are at the heart of A Rocha's mission. We work with churches and individuals too, inspiring and equipping them, and harnessing their enthusiasm as we care for God's world together. We also offer a consultancy service which provides quality conservation advice. In addition we support the wider family of A Rocha projects present in 18 countries.

Working together for a better environment, and for the preservation of the diversity and flourishing of living things, brings us back to the vision of God's creation as offered in the creation stories. We are the grown up and newly responsible Adams and Eves, who cannot break back in, but can make the landscape round about reflect the primordial beauty we remember as

1 See http://www.arocha.org/gb-en/whatwedo.html.

belonging to God's will. What does that mean, in practice? Here are some words from John, a park-keeper, about his view of his job:

John's story

Sounds funny but one of the best things that happened to me was when they found S... dead behind the shrubbery. He wanted to die in the park because he loved it and it meant something to him. It's the old people that the parks matter to. Keeping the parks nice is a way of saying we're civilised, isn't it? Over the years it's got more difficult, what with kids pulling up everything you plant and smashing things because they've got nothing else to do. But then you get kids from the schools coming and planting things and helping out. The beach has made a difference – that's like getting your history back and everybody owns something that people come from elsewhere to enjoy.

When you do the planting and the cutting and mowing it's hard work but it's making a better world for other people. I feel bad when people chuck litter on the grass and in the flower beds and when they let their dogs foul, but the council are pretty tough on them if they get caught. But once you wouldn't need to have penalties and laws. There was respect. I think what you're talking about [reconciliation] is about getting back respect for everybody and making your surroundings reflect that.

Reconciliation then, is a journey on which all of us are engaged. As we journey, we notice groups of Unreconciled people stalled on their journey by their circumstances, what is being done to them, or simply by their mental state. It is our task to reach out to them and to find the methods and processes that will allow them to start again and to join us as fellow pilgrims, to make progress towards that ultimate reconciliation which is in Christ. While we can be assured of this promise in Christ, and allow that assurance to build up our confidence and hope, that ultimate reconciliation is not finished within the time span of a human life. Our hope is in heaven, with the one who harrowed hell. Our death will be a birth through the good offices of the midwife of salvation, Christ himself. Or as T. S. Eliot puts it: 'in my end is my beginning'.

Conclusion

Jesus as midwife of our salvation

Jesus' resurrection represents to us the ultimate act of divine reconciliation. Walter Brueggemann calls the resurrection 'the ultimate energising of a new future' and he is right. [1]Jesus' resurrection transforms the notion that all that happens to us is that we grow old, sicken and die. His resurrection body is the vision of the eternity that God has prepared/is preparing/will prepare for us. So he is called by St Paul the 'second Adam', enabling the way back to God's perfect desire for the whole creation. Jesus' death and resurrection puts in the necessary moral and spiritual energy to deliver us from sin, evil and death, to make it possible for Christians to promise others the same release in a 'sure and certain hope'. So the events of Pentecost, for example, are profoundly reconciliatory, enabling people sundered by language and understanding to hear clearly the gracious words and works of God and undoing the chaotic symbol of Babel. The resurrection releases into the world a possibility for full healing and restoration. Responding to that opportunity results in the transforming effects of mission

Can reconciliation *ever* be achieved? If so, how can we know when we have reached a state of complete reconciliation? It is entirely possible that we can never know. Reconciliation is a process reaching into the deepest parts of human hearts, human lives and human communities. Its realisation depends on transformation, change and newness and on increasing understanding and realisation of the Kingdom of God. As human beings we can never perhaps experience full reconciliation, but there can be brief experiences of what it is like. Consequently, our partnership with God in the *missio dei* needs to be viewed from the perspective of eschatology, when we are able to come before God face to face and be fully known. But that eschatological hope can transfigure the value, meaning and purpose of all human life and make sense of our actions as Christians. Our task is to become pregnant with God's desire for a reconciled world and bring to birth the new things which enable it to come into being. Our mission feeds God's gestation, its embryology, the joyful birth of the life to come.

---

1 Walter Brueggemann, *Prophetic Imagination*, Augsberg: Fortress Press, 1978 p.106

Unreconciled? Resources

Notes for Group Leaders

This set of resources consists of an introductory session plus 10 other sessions for group work which are based on the topic chapters in this book. It is possible to mix and match the different topics according to the interests, age and abilities of the group.

Each topic works with the concept of the 'Unreconciled' – especially people untouched or overlooked by the usual processes of Christian reconciliation. The book contains a full explanation of this concept and is application to situations in human life.

Each session is laid out in the form of a learning journey with a suggested learning outcome for the group which will be facilitated by five forms of engagement, although these may also be mixed and matched or conducted over a period if time is short:

1. **Starting Out** – three possible activities are offered as a starting point for engagement with the topic and with suggestions for discussion and feedback

2. **Going Deeper** – a suggestion for Bible Study, including possibilities for mime and/or role play with particular emphasis on those who are members of an Unreconciled community within the text. Questions are provided to aid group discussion with some suggestions for particular engagement activities.

3. **Moving on** – a task for the group which requires the participants to engage with the local community in a way which raises awareness, provides interaction and fosters greater understanding of community issues. This item may require particular planning or be the focus of a day in itself.

4. **Resting on the Way** – an opportunity to reflect theologically on the topic in relation to the group's own experiences and with opportunities to look at how the local church might change and commit to a reconciling work or action as an outcome of the group's work.

5. **Gathering Up** – a suggestion for a concluding prayer drawing the threads of the topic together.

Leading the group will be helped by reading the related chapter in the main text and using the stories and illustrations provided. If you need further information about this resource you can contact Dr Anne Richards at: anne.richards@churchofengland.org. More ideas and resources are available at the MTAG website: www.spiritualjourneys.org.uk.

Session 1:
Order and disorder in the world

By the end of this session the group will have had opportunity to:

✤ Investigate order and disorder and become aware of the energy and work required to maintain order in our world (activity)

✤ Think about creation and destruction in relation to God's covenant with human beings (bible study)

✤ Carry out a simple reconciling task (restoring order) in the community;

✤ Reflect theologically on key questions about order and disorder

✤ Feed thoughts and ideas into prayer and reflection

1 Starting out – Activities

Investigating order and disorder

Choose from the selection below

A. Collect ten broken or dirty objects – damaged toys, a letter or photo torn in two, a broken flowerpot, a muddy and torn T-shirt, etc.

Divide people into three groups. Group one has cleaning materials, sello-tape, glue (not superglue) string, needle and thread, etc. Group two has pens, paints, glitter, ribbons and any other craft materials available.

Group 1's task is to repair 5 broken objects as best as they can in a time limit.

Group 2's task is to do something with their 5 broken objects using their creative materials in the time limit.

Group 3 has to judge the objects after treatment and say what they think about the results.

As a whole group discuss together: When is mending the better option? When is doing something completely different with a damaged object a better option? How did you feel about the task?

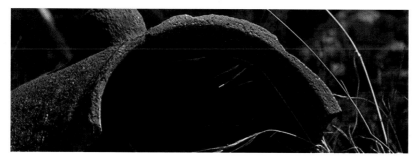

B. If you have a parent and toddler group or a school group, organize a children's party with lots of messy food. When the children have finished having fun take photographs of the dirty plates, tables and paper cups. Get a cleaning team to keep note of what materials are required to clean up and to restore order and take some more photographs of the cleaning process. Get the cleaning team to reflect on the effort it takes to put everything away and restore order. How long did it take? How many people were required? What resources did you need?

You can do this for any cleaning and tidying exercise, such as tiding away service sheets and hymn books after church or re-doing the flowers.

C. Find some simple jigsaws without too many pieces and divide into groups. Half the groups should make the jigsaws using the picture on the box. The other half should make their jigsaw without any reference to the picture. Compare notes on the process.

As a whole group, discuss: what difference does having a vision of what you're trying to achieve make to the process of reconstructing something broken?

2 Going Deeper – Bible study

You might want to read this passage aloud or organise it as a role play
Genesis 6.11–18; 8.21b–22; 9.8–17.

Now the earth was corrupt in God's sight and was full of violence. God saw how corrupt the earth had become, for all the people on earth had corrupted their ways. So God said to Noah, 'I am going to put an end to all people, for the earth is filled with violence because of them. I am surely going to destroy both them and the earth. So make yourself an ark of cypress wood; make rooms in it and coat it with pitch inside and out. This is how you are to build it: The ark is to be 450 feet long, 75 feet wide and 45 feet high. 16 Make a roof for it and finish the ark to within 18 inches of the top. Put a door in the side of the ark and make lower, middle and upper decks. I am going to bring

floodwaters on the earth to destroy all life under the heavens, every creature that has the breath of life in it. Everything on earth will perish. But I will establish my covenant with you, and you will enter the ark—you and your sons and your wife and your sons' wives with you.

The LORD smelled the pleasing aroma and said in his heart: 'Never again will I curse the ground because of man, even though every inclination of his heart is evil from childhood. And never again will I destroy all living creatures, as I have done.

> As long as the earth endures,
>   seedtime and harvest,
>   cold and heat,
>   summer and winter,
>   day and night
>   will never cease.

Then God said to Noah and to his sons with him: 'I now establish my covenant with you and with your descendants after you and with every living creature that was with you –the birds, the livestock and all the wild animals, all those that came out of the ark with you – every living creature on earth. I establish my covenant with you: Never again will all life be cut off by the waters of a flood; never again will there be a flood to destroy the earth.'

And God said, 'This is the sign of the covenant I am making between me and you and every living creature with you, a covenant for all generations to come: I have set my rainbow in the clouds, and it will be the sign of the covenant between me and the earth. Whenever I bring clouds over the earth and the rainbow appears in the clouds, I will remember my covenant between me and you and all living creatures of every kind. Never again will the waters become a flood to destroy all life. Whenever the rainbow appears in the clouds, I will see it and remember the everlasting covenant between God and all living creatures of every kind on the earth.'

So God said to Noah, 'This is the sign of the covenant I have established between me and all life on the earth.'

Some questions for discussion:

○ Who do you think are the Unreconciled in this story and what is their situation?

○ How do you feel about the phrase 'every inclination of his heart is evil'?

○ What do you feel about God's response to the Unreconciled?

○ Imagine you were Noah, what have you learned about God's wish to be reconciled with human beings? (For example: in pairs, one person could think about all the things Noah left behind and which are lost, while the other could 'count their blessings' at having been saved. What situations might make you want to count your blessings in your own life?)

3 Moving On – Task in the Community

Organize a litter picking day in your community. Take some photos of the exercise, including the amount of litter collected. What kinds of things did you find? How much of the litter could be recycled?

Reflect on where else in the community there is disorder, mess or pointless waste. Identify **one** thing where you could make a difference by spending time clearing up or reducing the waste and commit to doing it as a project.

4 Resting on the way – Theological reflection

Spend some time thinking about mess and disorder in our lives, in the Church, in the community and in the world. You might like to look at the stories offered in the introductory chapter in our book *Unreconciled?* It takes energy and effort to restore order and re-create God's vision for our world.

With these things in mind, consider these questions:

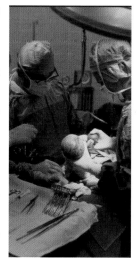

Where is the seed of new life? What gifts has God given us to counteract mess, waste and disorder in our situation?

How will we carry it? What resources will we need to make a difference in our situation?

Where can it be born? Identify **one** reconciling action we can commit to which will reduce or combat human waste and mess.

How can we nurture it? How can we support that reconciling action and make sure it follows through?

What will we hope to see? What will be changed at the end of the process and what difference should it have made?

5 Gathering up and going forward – Prayer

Lord,
We have torn your world apart;
it bleeds and reeks
with our restless lives.
Yet you remain patient,
stitching the fabric of the universe
into seamless beauty.
Teach us how to mend and make new;
teach us how to sew the tapestry
of your wonderful deeds.
Amen

Session 2: Humanity and God

By the end of this session the group will have had opportunity to:

+ Investigate ideas about God's reconciling work and our part in it

+ Think about human beings and God in the story of Jonah (bible study)

+ Carry out a simple reconciling task (befriending and inviting) in the community

+ Reflect theologically on key questions about God's call to us to partake in reconciling work

+ Feed thoughts and ideas into prayer and reflection

1 Starting Out – Activities

Choose from the selection below

A. Get one or more people from the caring professions in your community to talk to the group about why they do the jobs they do. Invite people such as a doctor or nurse, teacher, social worker, police officer or member of the clergy. What motivates people to work for others and what satisfaction is gained by it?

B. Talk in pairs about the people who live in your street, working out from your immediate next door neighbours.

○ How many people living near you do you *not* know anything about, and why?

○ How friendly is your neighbourhood?

○ What would it take to make more friends and meet more neighbours?

Glasgow tenements on black, 2006. ©Kenny Muir

C. Make a 'sorry' box out of an old tissue box or similar – a box with a small slit in it.

Encourage people to write a couple of lines about anything they regret or feel sorry for which has resulted in the loss of a relationship and post them in the sorry box. It does not have to be about something done wrong, just something regretted, like not having time to say goodbye before a person died. No-one is allowed to read another's contribution.

Spend some time in quiet reflection imagining the regret being read and being put right.

O What would have to happen for it to be put right?

O What would it feel like?

Involve as many people as possible in a decision about the complete disposal of the sorry box, so that the regrets are destroyed, praying for release from the pain caused by regret and unfinished business.

2 Going Deeper – Bible Study

You may like to have different people read sections or organise the story as a role play   **Matthew 12.38ff**

The word of the LORD came to Jonah son of Amittai: 'Go to the great city of Nineveh and preach against it, because its wickedness has come up before me.' But Jonah ran away from the LORD and Now the word of the Lord came to Jonah son of Amittai, saying 'Go at once to Nineveh, that great city, and cry out against it; for their wickedness has come up before me.' But Jonah set out to flee to Tarshish from the presence of the Lord. He went down to Joppa, where he found a ship bound for that port. After paying the fare, he went aboard and sailed for Tarshish to flee from the LORD. Then the LORD sent a great wind on the sea, and such a violent storm arose that the ship threatened to break up. All the sailors were afraid and each cried out to his own god. And they threw the cargo into the sea to lighten the ship.

But Jonah had gone below deck, where he lay down and fell into a deep sleep. The captain went to him and said, 'How can you sleep? Get up and call on your god! Maybe he will take notice of us, and we will not perish.' Then the sailors said to each other, 'Come, let us cast lots to find out who is responsible for this calamity.' They cast lots and the lot fell on Jonah. So they asked him, 'Tell us, who is responsible for making all this trouble for us? What do you do? Where do you come from? What is your country? From what people are you?' He answered, 'I am a Hebrew and I worship the LORD, the God of heaven, who made the sea and the land.' This terrified them and they asked, 'What have you done?' (They knew he was running away from the LORD, because he had already told them so.) The sea was getting rougher and rougher. So they asked him, 'What should we do to you to make the sea calm down for us?' 'Pick me up and throw me into the sea,' he replied, 'and it will become calm. I know that it is my fault that this great storm has come upon you.' Instead, the men did their best to row back to land. But they could not, for the sea grew even wilder than before. Then they cried to the LORD, 'O LORD, please do not let us die for taking this man's life. Do not hold us accountable for killing an innocent man, for you, O LORD, have done as you pleased.' Then they took Jonah and threw him overboard, and the raging sea grew calm. At this the men greatly feared the LORD, and they offered a sacrifice to the LORD and made vows to him. But the LORD provided a great fish to swallow Jonah, and Jonah was inside the fish three days and three nights.

From inside the fish Jonah prayed to the LORD his God. He said:

In my distress I called to the LORD,
    and he answered me.
    From the depths of the grave I called for help,
    and you listened to my cry.

You hurled me into the deep,
    into the very heart of the seas,
    and the currents swirled about me;
    all your waves and breakers
    swept over me'.

I said, 'I have been banished
    from your sight;
    yet I will look again
    toward your holy temple.

The engulfing waters threatened me,
    the deep surrounded me;
    seaweed was wrapped around my head.

To the roots of the mountains I sank down;
    the earth beneath barred me in forever.
    But you brought my life up from the pit,
    O LORD my God.

When my life was ebbing away,
    I remembered you, LORD,
    and my prayer rose to you,
    to your holy temple.

Those who cling to worthless idols
    forfeit the grace that could be theirs.

But I, with a song of thanksgiving,
    will sacrifice to you.
    What I have vowed I will make good.
    Salvation comes from the LORD.

And the LORD commanded the fish, and it vomited Jonah onto dry land.

Some questions to think about
- ○ Who do you think are the Unreconciled in this story and what is their situation?
- ○ How do you feel about 'those who cling to worthless idols forfeit the grace that could be theirs'? How do you think that statement relates to the world around us today?
- ○ Why do you think Jesus tells us that the sign of Jonah is the only sign that will be given to Jesus' generation? (Matthew 12.38; 16.4; Luke 11.29)
- ○ What can we learn from this story about how God calls us to do reconciling work among others?
- ○ Imagine you were one of the sailors, what would you learn from this experience? (For example: consider expressing this through your own drawing, diary, blog or prayer as if you were one of the sailors then share your thoughts with others in your group.)

3 Moving On – Task in the Community

Identify a facility in your community or local area where people might be cut off from their families eg prison, hospital, refugee or asylum seeker facility, shelter for the homeless, or residential home. Find out as much information as you can about it – how many people are there, how is it run, how it is funded, what sources of support the people there have. How can your group help foster genuine links with these people and help them feel more included?

4 Resting on the Way – Theological reflection

Read B's story to the group

B's story

I was 14 when I ran away from home. My parents didn't want a girl and were always favouring my two brothers. I never felt loved or wanted and I was always called 'stupid' or 'a waste of space'. I wasn't physically or sexually abused, I just got more and more unhappy and everyone just ignored me or forgot about me. Sometimes my brothers got meals, but I got forgotten. When I wanted to watch TV I was told to go to bed. If I tried to talk, my family pretended I wasn't there. So I ran away. At first I stayed with friends, but then they got fed up with me. I got drunk or took drugs. I started living on the street. I was so unhappy I wanted to die.

Ask the group how they feel about B's story

Her biggest lifeline is her mobile phone – in what ways can we use technology to overcome loneliness and loss of relationship?

With these things in mind, consider these questions:

Where is the seed of new life? What gifts has God given us to build better relationships in our own situation?

How will we carry it? What resources will we need to reach out to lonely and bereaved people in our situation and make the world around us neighbourly?

Where can it be born? Identify **one** reconciling action we can commit to which will help make the Unreconciled ones feel more included.

How can we nurture it? How can we support that reconciling action and make sure it follows through?

What will we hope to see? What will be changed at the end of this process and what difference should it have made?

5 Gathering Up – Prayer

Lord,
You are willing to wait forever
Holding out your hand
To those who are frozen into silence,
To those who have forgotten how to move,
To those who cannot believe in love,
To those who believe themselves unworthy.

We would be your hands in your loved world,
Speaking words of comfort into silence,
Helping the unmoving take first steps,
Teaching the unloved ones how to love,
Shining light on all who drift in shadow.
Amen

Session 3:
Speaking and Listening

By the end of this session the group will have had opportunity to:

+ Investigate ideas about how we use language to engage people or push people away

+ Think about the kind of language Jesus used (bible study)

+ Carry out a simple reconciling task based on careful use of words in the community

+ Reflect theologically on key questions about how we use our faith story as reconciling language

+ Feed thoughts and ideas into prayer and reflection

1 Starting out – Activities

Choose from the selection below

A. Exclamations!!! and questions???

Ask people to think about the last time they had a row with somebody. Did the other person say things which wounded them? Did they say anything deliberately hurtful? Even if they were really angry, were there things they were tempted to say but couldn't go that far? Ask the group to talk in pairs about what arguing makes you feel like inside. What kind of language do you need to make up after a row?

Now ask the group to think about a time when they were trying to make friends or to comfort somebody. What kind of things did they say? What does it feel like to try and reach out to someone you don't know very well? How do you keep a new conversation going?

You could write key words up on a flip chart or on post-its and compare the 'angry' words with the 'kind' words.

Or: an advertisement for mobile phones suggested that hearing an old song would make you remember an important relationship. What song would make you call someone you hadn't spoken to in a long time, and why?

B. On a board write up some headings:

Anger, hatred, blame, offensive language, blasphemy

Ask people to choose words which fit into the different categories (you can use magnetic words, post-its or similar if you like).

⭘ Ask people if they can say which of these words makes them feel particularly uncomfortable and why.

⭘ How do people feel when these words occur in TV programmes and films?

C. 'Jackal' language and 'Giraffe' Language

Look at this famous exchange between a politician: Michael Howard and a broadcaster: Jeremy Paxman. Two people might want to read it out.

Paxman: *Did you threaten to overule him?*
Howard: I was not entitled to instruct Derek Lewis and I did not instruct him.
Paxman: *Did you threaten to overule him?*
Howard: The truth of the matter is that Mr. Marriot was not suspended–
Paxman: *Did you threaten to overule him?*
Howard: I did not overule Derek Lewis–
Paxman: *Did you **threaten** to overule him?*
Howard: –I took advice on what I could or could not do–
Paxman: *Did you threaten to overule him?*
Howard: –and acted scrupulously in accordance with that advice. I did not overule Derek Lewis–
Paxman: *Did you threaten to overule him?*
Howard: –Mr. Marriot would not suspend him–
Paxman: *Did you threaten to overule him?*
Howard: I have accounted for my decision to dismiss Derek Lewis–
Paxman: *Did you threaten to overule him?*
Howard: –in great detail before the House of Commons–
Paxman: *I note that you're not answering the question whether you threatened to overule him.*
Howard: Well, the important aspect of this which it's very clear to bear in mind–
Paxman: *I'm sorry, I'm going to be frightfully rude but – I'm sorry – it's a straight yes-or-no question and a straight yes-or-no answer: did you threaten to overule him?*
Howard: I discussed the matter with Derek Lewis. I gave him the benefit of my opinion. I gave him the benefit of my opinion in strong language, but I did not instruct him because I was not, er, entitled to instruct him. I was entitled to express my opinion and that is what I did.
Paxman: *With respect, that is not answering the question of whether you threatened to overule him.*
Howard: It's dealing with the relevant point which was what I was entitled to do and what I was not entitled to do, and I have dealt with this in detail before the House of Commons and before the select committee.
Paxman: *But with respect you haven't answered the question of whether you threatened to overule him.*
Howard: Well, you see, the question is...

Jeremy Paxman never got a straight answer using this confrontational 'jackal language' technique.

- How else might it be possible to find out what the answer to the question was?
- What would it feel like to be questioned in this way?
- In what situations do people feel pressurized by a questioner (eg cold calls, salesmen, teachers, policemen etc).
- What do you feel about Jeremy Paxman's interviewing technique as opposed to the chat show host?
- Who do you think is the most sympathetic interviewer in the media, and why?

2 Going Deeper – Bible Study

You might want to ask some people to read the story aloud or organise it as a role play

John 4.1–30 ~ Jesus Talks With a Samaritan Woman

The Pharisees heard that Jesus was gaining and baptizing more disciples than John, although in fact it was not Jesus who baptized, but his disciples. When the Lord learned of this, he left Judea and went back once more to Galilee. Now he had to go through Samaria. So he came to a town in Samaria called Sychar, near the plot of ground Jacob had given to his son Joseph. Jacob's well was there, and Jesus, tired as he was from the journey, sat down by the well. It was about the sixth hour.

When a Samaritan woman came to draw water, Jesus said to her, 'Will you give me a drink?' (His disciples had gone into the town to buy food.) The Samaritan woman said to him, 'You are a Jew and I am a Samaritan woman. How can you ask me for a drink?' (For Jews do not associate with Samaritans.) Jesus answered her, 'If you knew the gift of God and who it is that asks you for a drink, you would have asked him and he would have given you living water.' 'Sir,' the woman said, 'you have nothing to draw with and the well is deep. Where can you get this living water? Are you greater than our father Jacob, who gave us the well and drank from it himself, as did also his sons and his flocks and herds?' Jesus answered, 'Everyone who drinks this water will be thirsty again, but whoever drinks the water I give him will never thirst. Indeed, the water I give him will become in him a spring of water welling up to eternal life.' The woman said to him, 'Sir, give me this water so that I won't get thirsty and have to keep coming here to draw water.' He told her, 'Go, call your husband and come back.' 'I have no husband,' she replied. Jesus said to her, 'You are right when you say you have no husband. The fact is, you have had five husbands, and the man you now have is not your husband. What you have just said is quite true.' 'Sir,' the woman said, 'I can see that you are a prophet. Our fathers worshipped on this mountain, but you Jews claim that the place where we must worship is in Jerusalem.' Jesus declared, 'Believe me, woman, a time is coming when you will worship the Father neither on this mountain nor in Jerusalem. You Samaritans worship what you do not know; we worship what we do know,

for salvation is from the Jews. Yet a time is coming and has now come when the true worshippers will worship the Father in spirit and truth, for they are the kind of worshippers the Father seeks. God is spirit, and his worshippers must worship in spirit and in truth.' The woman said, 'I know that Messiah' (called Christ) 'is coming. When he comes, he will explain everything to us.' Then Jesus declared, 'I who speak to you am he.'

Just then his disciples returned and were surprised to find him talking with a woman. But no one asked, 'What do you want?' or 'Why are you talking with her?' Then, leaving her water jar, the woman went back to the town and said to the people, 'Come, see a man who told me everything I ever did. Could this be the Christ?' They came out of the town and made their way toward him.

○ Who do you think are the Unreconciled in this story and what is their situation?
○ How does Jesus bridge the gap between types of people who never speak to one another?
○ How does Jesus use the basic everyday need of drawing water to teach the woman something important about God? How could we follow his example in our own situation?
○ Who do you think are 'the kind of worshippers the Father seeks'?
○ What can we learn from this story about how God calls us to do reconciling work among others?
○ Imagine you were the woman. What would you learn from this experience? (For example: in pairs work out what the woman might have said when she explained things to the villagers – you could develop a dialogue between her and her best friend; then read your dialogues to one another. Highlight what you have learnt from each other's accounts)

3 Moving On – Task in the Community

Design an event that will be welcoming and accessible to everyone in the community, regardless of faith or background. It could be a concert, book or poetry readings, a school or festival event, or something already in the calendar like a nativity play. Look carefully at the language of the event, what is being said, what is being said or sung together, what people are being asked to listen to. How does the language, music or drama of the event invite or prompt people to think about faith and how could the event provide space to allow people to explore faith questions and ideas?

4 Resting on the Way – Theological reflection

Read this passage to the group

'Why did I tell you those three stories?'

'Idunnomiss.'

Miss Massey hit him on both sides of the head, precisely with either hand, a word and a blow.

'God'

Smack!

'is'

Smack!

'love!'

Smack! Smack! Smack!

William Golding *Free Fall*

Do you think people sometimes experience the gospel in this extreme fashion?

With these things in mind, consider these questions

Where is the seed of new life? What gifts of communication has God given us to reach out to others in our own situation?

How will we carry it? What resources will we need to tell our story of faith sensitively to people in our community?

Where can it be born? Identify **one** reconciling action we can commit to which will help make the Unreconciled ones feel their voices have been heard.

How can we nurture it? How can we support that reconciling action and make sure it follows through?

What will we hope to see? What will be changed at the end of this process and what difference should it have made?

5 Gathering Up – Prayer

Lord,
You offer us a gracious speech,
a speech you have written in us
to be spoken to the world.
Help us not to twist your words,
not to say what suits us or gloss over
the message of your love,
but speak always of your gift to us,
tell everyone the joy of your good news.
Amen

Session 4: Lies and Truth

By the end of this session the group will have had opportunity to:

✦ Investigate ideas about how people are damaged by lies

✦ Think about how lies separate us from God's love (bible study)

✦ Carry out a simple reconciling task (sharing truth) in the community

✦ Reflect theologically on key questions about lies and truth

✦ Feed thoughts and ideas into prayer and reflection

1 Starting Out – Activities

Choose from the selection below

A. Truth and lies game

Give out some paper and pens.

Ask the group to write two truths and a lie about themselves. Choose things that might convince others that truth is a lie and the lie is true.

For example: I was born in London (true), I have four sisters (true), I am a vegetarian (false)

In pairs, get people to discuss their true/untrue statements with each other with the task of getting your partner to think your lie is true and one of your true statements is false. Don't own up at this stage even if the other person has guessed correctly.

As a whole group, get each person to read out their statements and get the group to vote true or false.

Gather feedback about the ease or difficulty of spotting truth and lies.

B. Stereotypes

Find some jokes in a book or on the internet which suggest:
- ○ Irish people are stupid;
- ○ Scots people are mean;
- ○ Blonde women are stupid;
- ○ Jewish mothers are obsessed with their sons.

Now consider the following statements:
- ○ Black people are inferior to white people
- ○ Women are inferior to men
- ○ Asylum seekers and refugees are scroungers
- ○ Disabled people are better off dead

Ask the group to discuss: what's the difference between a joke and dangerous devaluing of human beings?

C. Consider this story

Alhaji was a child soldier in Sierra Leone. He has been able to move from soldier to peace maker and to tell his story to the UN Security Council.

Alhaji's story

In 1997, when I was 10 years old, I went on Christmas holiday to my uncle,' Alhaji told the Security Council. 'During the second week, we heard that the rebels were 10 miles away from us. We ran into the bush to hide. On the second night, my elder brother and I went to look for water to do the cooking, and we ran into the rebels. We were taken back to our village where we were tied up, beaten and kept in the hot burning sun. Many houses were burnt down and people killed. My uncle was later killed.

That same night we were ordered by the rebels to go with them to their base behind Kabala Town. We walked for about 10 days in the bush, resting for only a few hours in between, mostly on empty stomachs. On arrival we were trained for a week to shoot and dismantle AK47 guns. Thereafter I was used to fighting. We killed people, burnt down houses, destroyed properties and cut limbs. But most of the time I went on food raids and did domestic work for my commander's wife. This is because I was so skinny.

In January 2000, two years after my capture, UN peacekeepers met with our commander to explain the DDR [Disarmament, Demobilization and Re-integration] process. Within two days more than 250 children were released. We were taken to a care centre in Lunsar and I was later handed over to [the local non-governmental organization] Caritas Makeni for care and protection ...

I was put in a community school together with other children. The children were not friendly to us. They kept calling us 'rebel children'. So Caritas had several meetings with various community people to forgive and accept us. This worked very well, because at the end of the year a woman from the community agreed to foster me. I am still living with her, because my family has not been found yet ...

I thank you for inviting me to tell my story on behalf of my brothers and sisters in Sierra Leone and in other countries at war. I hope that in all countries the government and the UN will listen to children and take our words into account. We want a better life. We want peace. We are counting on your continued support for this. [1] With permission of UNICEF: www.unicef.org

1 This story can be found at : http://www.unicef.org/voy/explore/rights/explore_233.html.

Find other such stories of people who have been forced to live a lie. Make a list of what kinds of liberating work can dispel the lie and allow the truth to be revealed. Are any such people present in our communities? If so, what can be done to help them?

2 Going Deeper – Bible Study

Luke 22.54–62 – Peter denies Jesus

You can get people to read the story aloud or organise it as a role play
Then seizing him, they led him away and took him into the house of the high priest. Peter followed at a distance. But when they had kindled a fire in the middle of the courtyard and had sat down together, Peter sat down with them. A servant girl saw him seated there in the firelight. She looked closely at him and said, 'This man was with him.'

But he denied it. 'Woman, I don't know him,' he said.

A little later someone else saw him and said, 'You also are one of them.' 'Man, I am not!' Peter replied.

About an hour later another asserted, 'Certainly this fellow was with him, for he is a Galilean.'

Peter replied, 'Man, I don't know what you're talking about!' Just as he was speaking, the rooster crowed. The Lord turned and looked straight at Peter. Then Peter remembered the word the Lord had spoken to him: 'Before the rooster crows today, you will disown me three times.' And he went outside and wept bitterly.

○ How do you think concealing the truth affects Peter in this story?
○ Peter denies categorically that he is associated with Jesus, even though those around him suspect that he is a disciple. How can we help those who are afraid to acknowledge Jesus to do so safely and freely? Can you think of situations in different countries or under other regimes where it might be necessary or permitted to conceal the truth of discipleship/ commitment to Christ ?
○ What do you think is the significance of Jesus knowing that Peter will deny him?
○ What can we learn from this story about how God calls us to tell the truth about Christian faith?
○ Imagine you were Peter, how do you think you would have been changed by this experience? (For example: role play a conversation with John and Peter through which John finds out what has happened to Peter. What might John say to help Peter? OR do a similar exercise with Mary Magdalene and Peter. Consider other situations where people 'betray' someone close to them eg when people write memoirs or give interviews about their relationships. Talk together about differences and similarities in the situations and the betrayed person's responses)

3 Moving On – Task in the Community

Invite any people you know from your local community who have to deal with issues of lies and truth to talk about the difficulties in sorting out what people say. Such people could include police officers, teachers, social workers or magistrates. Discuss with them how they make decisions about truth and how they act on those decisions.

4 Resting on the Way – Theological reflection

Read this story to the group

Grace's story

It started at school. Somebody who didn't like me started a rumour that I stole a CD from a shop. I denied it to anyone who asked, but after a week everyone believed I was stealing CDs. Some people started pestering me to get *them* CDs. Soon it was everywhere and when someone lost some money I got blamed as a thief. I was going mad. My teacher asked me if I was stealing things and I got flustered and upset because I couldn't explain that I wasn't and hadn't done anything wrong. Even when the rumour got so out of hand that the first person said it was made up, no one believed her. In everyone's mind I was a thief. It made my life a misery.

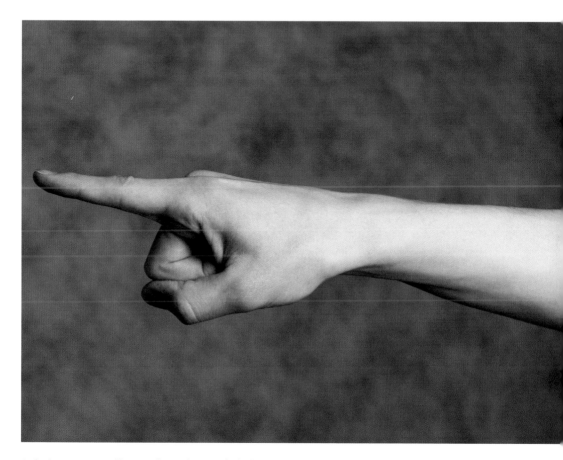

Ask the group to discuss: how do you feel about Grace's story?

With these things in mind, consider these questions

Where is the seed of new life? What gifts has God given us to tell the truth about the people in our community?

How will we carry it? What resources will we need to rectify injustice caused by lies and concealment of the truth?

Where can it be born? Identify **one** reconciling action we can commit to which will help make the Unreconciled ones feel their story has been told.

How can we nurture it? How can you support that reconciling action and make sure it follows through?

What will we hope to see? What will be changed at the end of this process and what difference should it have made?

5 Gathering Up – Prayer

Lord,
We pray for all those held captive by untruth,
People who have been lied to,
People who have been lied about,
People who have been forced to live a lie every day.

Your way is truth and it is life;
Help us to break down the web of lies,
To clear a space for grief and painful stories,
So that your light and peace
Can find a new place in the hearts of all.
Amen

Session 5:
Victimised and Victimisers

By the end of this session the group will have had opportunity to:

+ Investigate ideas about victimhood and the place of the victimised among the Unreconciled

+ Think about the victimised and victimisers in scripture (bible study)

+ Carry out a simple reconciling task (victim support) in the community

+ Reflect theologically on key questions about God's call to us to partake in reconciling work among the victimised and victimisers

+ Feed thoughts and ideas into prayer and reflection

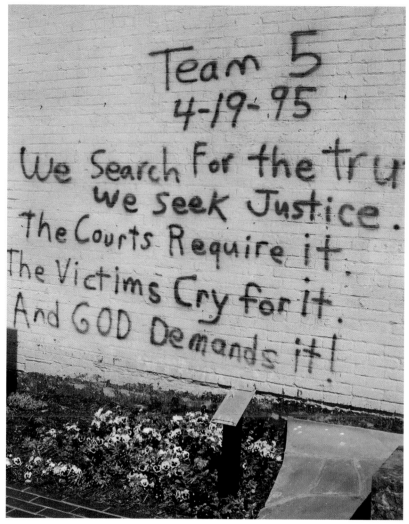

Firefighters Message
at Oklahoma City
National Memoria.

1 Starting out – Activities

Choose from the selection below

A. Make a list of people who can be considered 'victims' in our society, using newspapers and/or the internet. How many different kinds of 'victims' are there? Also look up what kind of victim support groups exist and investigate if any are active in your area.

B. If anyone in your community is a Samaritan, invite them to speak about their experiences of volunteer work. Otherwise consider their mission and vision statement:

Vision Mission and Values

The Vision
Samaritans Vision is that fewer people die by suicide.

The Mission
We work to achieve this Vision by making it our Mission to alleviate emotional distress and reduce the incidence of suicide feelings and suicidal behaviour.

We do this by:
- ○ Being available 24 hours a day to provide emotional support for people who are experiencing feelings of emotional distress or despair, including those which may lead to suicide
- ○ Reaching out to high risk groups and communities to reduce the risk of suicide
- ○ Working in partnership with other organisations, agencies and experts
- ○ Influencing public policy and raising awareness of the challenges of reducing suicide

The Values

We are committed to the following values:

○ Listening, because exploring feelings alleviates distress and helps people to reach a better understanding of their situation and the options open to them

○ Confidentiality, because if people feel safe, they are more likely to be open about their feelings

○ People making their own decisions wherever possible, because we believe that people have the right to find their own solution and telling people what to do takes responsibility away from them

○ Being non-judgemental, because we want people to be able to talk to us without fear of prejudice or rejection

○ Human contact, because giving people time, undivided attention and empathy meets a fundamental emotional need and reduces distress and despair [1]

　　○ How does this mission and these values engage with the world of the Unreconciled?

　　○ Would you want to add anything else to the engagement with despairing people?

C. Watch clips from a film such as *The Others*. **Some questions about the film might include:**

○ What does *The Others* teach us about the Unreconciled state of 'victims'?

○ In the story, Nicole Kidman's character believes herself victimised by outside forces or ghosts. What effect does her behaviour have on those around her?

○ How do you think her family could be helped or saved?

1 www.samaritans.org/about_samaritans/governance_and_history/our_mission.aspx

○ What does the background of war have to do with the state of the people in the film?

○ In what ways might you feel sorry for Nicole Kidman's character?

2 Going Deeper – Bible Study

You might want to read this passage aloud or organise it as a mime or dance   Isaiah 53.1–12

He was despised and rejected by men,
> a man of sorrows, and familiar with suffering.
> Like one from whom men hide their faces
> he was despised, and we esteemed him not.

Surely he took up our infirmities
> and carried our sorrows,
> yet we considered him stricken by God,
> smitten by him, and afflicted.

But he was pierced for our transgressions,
> he was crushed for our iniquities;
> the punishment that brought us peace was upon him,
> and by his wounds we are healed.

We all, like sheep, have gone astray,
> each of us has turned to his own way;
> and the LORD has laid on him
> the iniquity of us all.

He was oppressed and afflicted,
  yet he did not open his mouth;
  he was led like a lamb to the slaughter,
  and as a sheep before her shearers is silent,
  so he did not open his mouth.

By oppression and judgment he was taken away.
  And who can speak of his descendants?
  For he was cut off from the land of the living;
  for the transgression of my people he was stricken.

He was assigned a grave with the wicked,
  and with the rich in his death,
  though he had done no violence,
  nor was any deceit in his mouth.

Yet it was the LORD's will to crush him and cause him to suffer,
  and though the LORD makes his life a guilt offering,
  he will see his offspring and prolong his days,
  and the will of the LORD will prosper in his hand.

After the suffering of his soul,
  he will see the light of life and be satisfied ;
  by his knowledge my righteous servant will justify many,
  and he will bear their iniquities.

Therefore I will give him a portion among the great,
  and he will divide the spoils with the strong,
  because he poured out his life unto death,
  and was numbered with the transgressors.
  For he bore the sin of many,
  and made intercession for the transgressors.

○ Who is the Unreconciled one in this passage and what is his situation?
○ The passage states that 'the punishment that brought us peace was upon
  him' How do you feel about a God who requires punishment for peace?
  How does this statement relate to the world around us today?
○ How does this passage prefigure what happened to Jesus?
○ What can we learn from this story about God's own reconciling work?
○ How do you think a scapegoat would feel? See the rite described in
  Leviticus 16.20–22. Also see John 1.29 and Hebrews chs 9–10. (For
  example: ask each member of the group to EITHER draw a sketch to
  show how a person might express through their body position that they
  are 'unreconciled' OR to show this through their own body posture. Then
  invite other members of the group to share what this communicates to
  them, eg rejection, loneliness, anger etc)

3 Moving on – Task in the Community

Make contact with any victim support groups in your local area. Find what they do and look at how your local church or fellowship could help to support their activities.

4 Resting on the Way – Theological reflection

Read this story to the group

A Bombers' story

I and thousands like me have forsaken everything for what we believe. Our driving motivation doesn't come from tangible commodities that this world has to offer. Your democratically elected Governments continuously perpetuate atrocities against my people all over the world, and your support of them makes you directly responsible. Until we feel security, you will be our targets and until you stop the bombing, gassing, imprisonment and torture of my people, we will not stop this fight. We are at war and I'm a soldier, now you too will taste the reality of this situation.

Mohammed Siddique Khan, one of the London suicide bombers of 7 July 2005[1]

Rescue workers help an injured police official injured in bomb explosion in Mathra, at Lady Reading hospital on February 08, 2011 in Peshawar, Pakistan.

Ask the group to discuss: in your view, was Mohammed Siddique Khan one of the victimised, a victimiser or both?

With these things in mind, consider these questions

Where is the seed of new life? What gifts has God given us to help us care for the victimised and understand the behaviour of victimisers?

How will we carry it? What resources will we need to reach out to the victimised and restore them to equality with all other people?

Where can it be born? Identify **one** reconciling action we can commit to which will help improve the lives of victimised people in our communities.

How can we nurture it? How can we support that reconciling action and make sure it follows through?

What will we hope to see? What will be changed at the end of this process and what difference should it have made?

5 Gathering Up – Prayer

Lord,
You entered the world of the Unreconciled
You were despised and rejected
Terrible things were done to you
No one fought to save you
And you did not save yourself.

Yet through your suffering
Others believed
And you promised the criminal
He would walk with you in Paradise.

Help us to raise the victimised
From their place of desolation
And give them the hope of your risen glory.
Amen

Christ in Glory, Graham Sutherland tapestry, in Coventry Cathedral, Coventry, England by David Jones

Session 6:
Punishment and Liberation

By the end of this session the group will have had opportunity to:

✚ Investigate ideas about the prison community as the Unreconciled

✚ Think about issues of punishment and restoration in scripture (bible study)

✚ Carry out a simple reconciling task (reaching out to offenders and victims) in the community

✚ Reflect theologically on key questions about God's call to us to partake in reconciling work among offenders

✚ Feed thoughts and ideas into prayer and reflection

1 Starting out – Activities

Choose from the selection below

A. Invite a member of the local police force, probation officer or magistrate to give their account of the effects of crime on both offenders and victims of crime. Find out what their views are on how the issues of punishment and liberation should be handled.

B. Ask the group if anyone or anyone they know has been the object of a crime. What was it like and how did they feel about what happened? Was the perpetrator caught and if so how did that feel?

C. Ask the group to discuss the issue of punishment. Is there such a thing as an appropriate or satisfactory punishment?

2 Going Deeper – Bible Study

You might want to read this passage aloud or organise it as a role play

Matthew 14.22–33 – Jesus Walks on the Water

Immediately Jesus made the disciples get into the boat and go on ahead of him to the other side, while he dismissed the crowd. After he had dismissed them, he went up on a mountainside by himself to pray. When evening came, he was there alone, but the boat was already a considerable distance from land, buffeted by the waves because the wind was against it.

During the fourth watch of the night Jesus went out to them, walking on the lake. When the disciples saw him walking on the lake, they were terrified. 'It's a ghost,' they said, and cried out in fear.

But Jesus immediately said to them: 'Take courage! It is I. Don't be afraid.'

'Lord, if it's you,' Peter replied, 'tell me to come to you on the water.'

'Come,' he said.

Then Peter got down out of the boat, walked on the water and came toward Jesus. But when he saw the wind, he was afraid and, beginning to sink, cried out, 'Lord, save me!'

Immediately Jesus reached out his hand and caught him. 'You of little faith,' he said, 'why did you doubt?'

And when they climbed into the boat, the wind died down. Then those who were in the boat worshipped him, saying, 'Truly you are the Son of God.'

○ Who is the Unreconciled one in this passage and what is his situation?

○ Jesus says 'you of little faith, why did you doubt?' What do you think this means and how does this statement relate to the world around us today?

○ Why do you think prisoners identify especially with this passage?

○ What can we learn from this story about God's own reconciling work?

○ Imagine you were Peter. How do you think he felt when he started to drown? OR imagine you were one of the other disciples. How did you feel when you saw Peter sinking? (Another possibility would be for the group to consider what soundtrack could accompany the story – what sort of music would you choose to illustrate it and why?)

3 Moving On – Task in the Community

Set up an Amnesty Day or Event which could allow people to give up weapons, leave prayers for people they have hurt, or teach people about the sacrament of reconciliation. Alternatively set up a display to make people aware of charities and projects aimed at helping prisoners and victims of crime. The charity Amnesty also has an annual Greetings Card Campaign in which people can send greetings to people all over the world who are in prison or suffering human rights abuses (see www.amnesty.org.uk/gcc).

Amnesty logo reproduced with permission: www.amnesty.org.uk

4 Resting on the Way – Theological reflection

Read this story to the group

A man joined the BNP as a candidate because he does not feel that the murderer of his teenaged son received a long enough sentence. He said that this was the only way he could achieve justice for his son.

Ask the group to discuss: what does this story tell us about the nature of our society? What do you think God's way would be?

With these things in mind, consider these questions

Where is the seed of new life? What gifts has God given us to build better relationships between offenders and victims of crime?

How will we carry it? What resources will we need to reach out to offenders and victims of crime in our own situation?

Where can it be born? Identify **one** reconciling action we can commit to which will help the cause of Restorative Justice.

How can we nurture it? How can we support that reconciling action and make sure it follows through?

What will we hope to see? What will be changed at the end of it and what difference should it have made?

5 Gathering Up – Prayer

Lord,
When did we ever see you naked,
Hungry or thirsty,
Shivering in corners,
Locked in a cell?

Surely you are Lord of all,
You are not to be found
Among the thieves, the murderers
The heroin addicts and among all
That you are not?

Help us to see that Love
Makes you cast off your cloak,
Give away your food,
Walk into prison

To the utmost depths.
Help us to remember you
And so remember all
You would bring back to light.
Amen

Session 7:
Wounds and Healing

By the end of this session the group will have had opportunity to:

✚   **Investigate ideas about God's desire to heal what is wounded**

✚   **Think about Jesus' healing miracles (bible study)**

✚   **Carry out a simple reconciling task (healing service) in the community**

✚   **Reflect theologically on key questions about God's call to us to partake in healing work**

✚   **Feed thoughts and ideas into prayer and reflection**

1 Starting Out – Activities

Choose from the selection below

A. Ask the group to share any experiences of being in hospital. What was it like to be a patient and what was it like to go home again?

B. Ask people to consider the cases of children helped by the charity Facing the World (see http://www.facingtheworld.net). How would you feel if it was your child who was cast out because they looked different?

C. Ask people to share any stories of living with chronic disease such as asthma, arthritis, diabetes, etc. What does healing mean in the context of an ongoing but non life threatening health problem? What relationship does living with disease or disability have to healing?

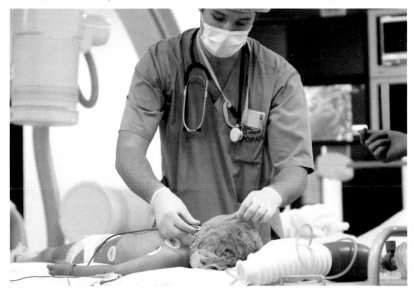

Doctors prepare to operate on a child diagnosed with congenital heart disease within the II Ukrainian Medical Forum on October 11, 2007 in Kyiv, Ukraine

2 Going Deeper – Bible Study

You might want to read this passage aloud or organise it as a role play

Luke 8.26–33

They sailed to the region of the Gerasenes, which is across the lake from Galilee. When Jesus stepped ashore, he was met by a demon-possessed man from the town. For a long time this man had not worn clothes or lived in a house, but had lived in the tombs. When he saw Jesus, he cried out and fell at his feet, shouting at the top of his voice, 'What do you want with me, Jesus, Son of the Most High God? I beg you, don't torture me!' For Jesus had commanded the evil spirit to come out of the man. Many times it had seized him, and though he was chained hand and foot and kept under guard, he had broken his chains and had been driven by the demon into solitary places.

Jesus asked him, 'What is your name?'

'Legion,' he replied, because many demons had gone into him. And they begged him repeatedly not to order them to go into the Abyss.

A large herd of pigs was feeding there on the hillside. The demons begged Jesus to let them go into them, and he gave them permission. When the demons came out of the man, they went into the pigs, and the herd rushed down the steep bank into the lake and was drowned.

When those tending the pigs saw what had happened, they ran off and reported this in the town and countryside, and the people went out to see what had happened. When they came to Jesus, they found the man from whom the demons had gone out, sitting at Jesus' feet, dressed and in his right mind; and they were afraid. Those who had seen it told the people how the demon-possessed man had been cured. Then all the people of the region of the Gerasenes asked Jesus to leave them, because they were overcome with fear. So he got into the boat and left.

The man from whom the demons had gone out begged to go with him, but Jesus sent him away, saying, 'Return home and tell how much God has done for you.' So the man went away and told all over town how much Jesus had done for him.

○ Who is the Unreconciled in this story and what is his situation?
○ Why is everyone so frightened of what Jesus did? How does that statement relate to the world around us today?
○ What mission does Jesus give the healed man and what lesson can we learn from it?
○ What can you learn from this story about how God calls us to do reconciling work among others?
○ Imagine you were the Gerasene demoniac. What do you think he learned from this experience? (For example: divide a sheet of paper in two. Use some abstract colours to express how the man might have felt before he met Jesus and after he was healed. Show each other your work and invite others to say what your colours suggest to them. OR together write a short drama about the man's return to the village and how he would explain what had happened to him).

3 Moving On – Task in the Community
Organise a service to pray for healing in the community.

4 Resting on the Way – Theological reflection

Read this story to the group

Anita (aged 12)

I had an accident in the kitchen and knocked a saucepan of boiling water over me. My arms, neck and parts of my face were all splashed and burned. I had to spend a lot of time in hospital getting skin grafts, but I still had loads of scars. I hated the pain but I hated the sight of myself more.

One day, when I was in hospital a 'celebrity' came round to visit all the children. We were all excited. He came and gave out toys and gifts and had a chat with everyone. When he came to me he said 'Have you got a boyfriend? I bet a pretty girl like you would have a boyfriend'. Thing was, I saw him wince when he looked at my face. I knew he was trying to be nice but it was completely the wrong thing to say. I didn't have a boyfriend and was convinced at the time that no one would ever want me. That night I pulled the bandages off my arm and pulled out the stitches. I couldn't see the point of going on.

A woman who was burned in a house fire now works for the Peter Hughes Burn Foundation in Australia providing counselling and support for the victims of the bush fires.

Ask the group to discuss what role wounds and healing have to play in self-esteem and personal identity.

With these things in mind, consider these questions
Where is the seed of new life? What gifts has God given us to offer Christian healing in our own situation?
How will we carry it? What resources will we need to make that healing ministry available in our situation?

Where can it be born? Identify one healing action we can commit to which will help make the Unreconciled ones feel their wounds are being addressed.
How can we nurture it? How can we support that reconciling action and make sure it follows through?
What will we hope to see? What will be changed at the end of this process and what difference should it have made?

5 Gathering Up – Prayer

Prayer to the Compassionate Christ[1]
Lord Jesus,
We do not want to suffer alone or for no purpose.
Remind us often that you experienced the weaknesses, trials and
     sufferings of being human – and that you did that to save us.
May your sufferings and wounds bring us life, healing and hope even now.
We press our open wounds to your precious wounds
That we may be united to you and to your will for us.
May we receive your comfort, compassion and courage
And may we bring comfort, compassion and courage to others.
Pour your healing love into us and through us may it also bless and heal
     others.
Amen

---

1 Prayer courtesy Andrew Brookes OP.

Session 8: Otherness and Self

By the end of this session the group will have had opportunity to:

+ Investigate ideas about ourselves in relation to the Other

+ Think about Unreconciled peoples becoming neighbours (bible study)

+ Carry out a simple reconciling task (befriending and inviting) in the community

+ Reflect theologically on key questions about God's call to us to partake in reconciling work towards the Other

+ Feed thoughts and ideas into prayer and reflection

1 Starting Out – Activities

Choose from the selection below

A. Ask the group to imagine life in heaven and to list who they would like to see there. Who is not included in such a picture and why not?

B. Ask the group to share holiday and travel experiences in foreign countries, perhaps by sharing photographs or a video. What was strange and unfamiliar about new places? What was it like to learn a language or make new friends?

C. Ask the group to divide into pairs and imagine what it might be like to be locked in a room with a stranger. While you are waiting to be let out, what would you talk about to break the silence? What would you be willing to share?

2 Going Deeper – Bible Study

You might want to read this passage aloud or organise it as a role play

Luke 10.30–37 – Good Samaritan

In reply Jesus said: 'A man was going down from Jerusalem to Jericho, when he fell into the hands of robbers. They stripped him of his clothes, beat him and went away, leaving him half dead. A priest happened to be going down the same road, and when he saw the man, he passed by on the other side. So too, a Levite, when he came to the place and saw him, passed by on the other side. But a Samaritan, as he travelled, came where the man was; and when he saw him, he took pity on him. He went to him and bandaged his wounds, pouring on oil and wine. Then he put the man on his own donkey, took him to an inn and took care of him. The next day he took out two silver coins and gave them to the innkeeper. 'Look after him,' he said, 'and when I return, I will reimburse you for any extra expense you may have.'

'Which of these three do you think was a neighbour to the man who fell into the hands of robbers?'

The expert in the law replied, 'The one who had mercy on him.' Jesus told him, 'Go and do likewise.'

○ Who are the Unreconciled in this story and what is their situation?
○ What do you think the injured man felt about being ignored and then helped by an 'enemy'?
○ How do you think people reacted when asked who was truly the injured man's neighbour?
○ What can you learn from this story about how God calls us to do reconciling work among others?
○ Imagine you were the priest or the Levite – what were you thinking when you ignored the injured man? (OR: imagine the Levite catches up with the priest and they talk about what they have seen and why they

didn't help. Improvise their conversation. Did this draw them together or push them apart?)

3 Moving On – Task in the Community

Identify a group of Other in the local situation or in the wider community. These could be people of another faith, travellers or asylum seekers for example. Find out all you can about them and their way of life, their beliefs and customs. Then ask half the group to make a presentation acting as advocates for the Others if they want to use the church hall, send their children to the Church school, receive help or benefits from the church.

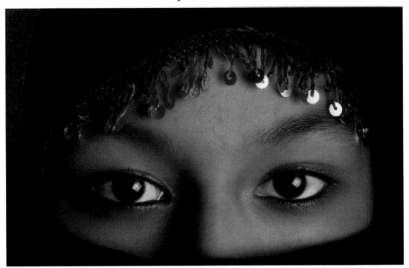

4 Resting on the way – Theological reflection

You might like to read this story to the group

An elderly woman put an advertisement in a local paper to rent one of her spare rooms to a female lodger. She was very surprised when all the people who replied were foreign students. She opted for a young woman from Taiwan who startled the houseowner by cooking unfamiliar dishes in the kitchen and meditating in the living room. As time went on, the houseowner came to look forward to the smell of cooking and was delighted to be invited to share meals with her young lodger. The younger woman also taught her to meditate when she felt worried or upset so that she felt calmer and more able to cope. In return the houseowner taught the student to knit and helped her with her English.

Ask the group to discuss what we could offer to a visitor from another country if they came to stay in our homes on an exchange visit. What would you learn on the exchange?

With these things in mind, consider these questions

Where is the seed of new life? What gifts has God given us to build better relationships with those unlike ourselves?

How will we carry it? What resources will we need to reach out to the Other in your own situation and make the world around us neighbourly?

Where can it be born? Identify **one** reconciling action we can commit to which will help make the Others around us feel more included.

How can we nurture it? How can we support that reconciling action and make sure it follows through?

What will we hope to see? What will be changed at the end of this process and what difference should it have made?

5 Gathering Up – Prayer

Lord,
Help us to turn strangers into friends,
Learning each other's language
Knowing each other's culture,
Finding out what makes them love, laugh, cry,
Turn to us in time of need.
Help us always to see the Other
As a treasure house of riches
Put there by you for us to discover
And may they find treasure in us, too.
Amen

Session 9:
Separation and Unity

By the end of this session the group will have had opportunity to:

✦ Investigate the things which separate us from neighbour

✦ Think about issues of separation and unity in scripture (bible study)

✦ Carry out a simple reconciling task (overcoming history) in the community

✦ Reflect theologically on key questions about God's call to us to work for unity

✦ Feed thoughts and ideas into prayer and reflection

1 Starting Out – Activities

Choose from the selection below

A. Ask the group beforehand to talk to people in your neighbourhood about where they see divisions in your community, or look at local newspapers to identify those divisions. Any there any issues which your local newspapers are missing – could you write about these to your local paper to highlight them?

B. Ask the group to share stories of any people in their families, neighbours or friends who stopped talking to them, lost contact with them or fell out with them in some way. How did the separation happen and what did it take to heal the breach? What happens in those cases where separations never get reconciled?

C. Ask the group to consider where diversity adds to richness in the community. What is enjoyable about encountering different lifestyles, cultures, religions, etc? Are there occasions where diversity is too much to take in or cope with, or becomes confusing or even alienating?

2 Going Deeper – Bible Study

You might want to read this passage aloud

Ephesians 2.11–22 – One in Christ

Therefore, remember that formerly you who are Gentiles by birth and called 'uncircumcised' by those who call themselves 'the circumcision' (that done in the body by the hands of men)— remember that at that time you were separate from Christ, excluded from citizenship in Israel and foreigners to the covenants of the promise, without hope and without God in the world. But now in Christ Jesus you who once were far away have been brought near through the blood of Christ.

For he himself is our peace, who has made the two one and has destroyed the barrier, the dividing wall of hostility, by abolishing in his flesh the law with its commandments and regulations. His purpose was to create in himself one new man out of the two, thus making peace, and in this one body to reconcile both of them to God through the cross, by which he put to death their hostility. He came and preached peace to you who were far away and peace to those who were near. For through him we both have access to the Father by one Spirit.

Consequently, you are no longer foreigners and aliens, but fellow citizens with God's people and members of God's household, built on the foundation of the apostles and prophets, with Christ Jesus himself as the chief cornerstone. In him the whole building is joined together and rises

to become a holy temple in the Lord. And in him you too are being built together to become a dwelling in which God lives by his Spirit.

○ Who are the Unreconciled in this passage and what is their situation?

○ What kinds of problems are there in making two very difficult communities become one? How does that statement relate to the world around us today?

○ What has to happen before people no longer feel 'foreign' or 'alien' in a community?

○ What can we learn from this story about how God calls us to do reconciling work among others?

○ Imagine you were part of the early Christian communities. What would be your thoughts about this vision of common fellowship? (For example, EITHER work out a dialogue between a Jew and a Greek hearing this in Ephesus – what might they say to each other about their feelings and the practical challenges, OR do the same for a modern division within the church. OR imagine you are in a charge of a reconciliation meeting between the Jew and the Greek. How would you get them to talk honestly about the damage each has done to the other? Create a structure for the conversation and see where it goes.

3 Moving On – Task in the Community

Ask the group to find time to attend a service or event in a church of another denomination. Ask the group later to compare experiences. Who did you meet? What was the service or the event like? What things felt familiar and what strange. Would you want to go back and why?

4 Resting on the Way – Theological reflection

Have a look at the website of the St Ethelburga's centre for peace and reconciliation at www.stethelburgas.org. Using the stories and resources on the site think about how your church could create a vision or mission statement which would commit your Christian community to greater understanding of your others within your own wider neighbourhood.

Spend some time thinking about how your vision statement could be realised through practical initiatives. These could be ecumenical events, inter-faith initiatives, community based partnerships, or other collaborations which suit your own community.

OR spend some time thinking about how you could become better neighbours to those around you.

With these things in mind, consider these questions

Where is the seed of new life? What gifts has God given us to overcome long standing barriers between neighbours and communities?

How will we carry it? What resources will we need to reach out to the alienated and foreign people in our own situation?

Where can it be born? Identify **one** reconciling action we can commit to which will help make the Unreconciled ones feel more included.

How can we nurture it? How can we support that reconciling action and make sure it follows through?

What will we hope to see? What will be changed at the end of this process and what difference should it have made?

5 Gathering Up – Prayer

Lord,
Help us to overcome our histories,
Our long ago memories of rights and wrongs,
The people we feared, the people we shunned.
Help us to see you in everyone we meet,
To assume that goodness lives in every person
And find beyond our familiar friends and family,
Neighbours of all kinds waiting to be embraced.
Amen

Session 10:
Condemnation and Forgiveness

By the end of this session the group will have had opportunity to:

+ Investigate ideas about condemnation and forgiveness in our own lives

+ Think about condemnation and forgiveness in scripture (bible study)

+ Carry out a simple reconciling task (forgiveness project) in the community

+ Reflect theologically on key questions about God's call to us to understand and effect forgiveness

+ Feed thoughts and ideas into prayer and reflection

1 Starting Out – Activities

Choose from the selection below

A. Ask the group to divide into pairs and discuss whether they have ever been accused of something they didn't do, or were at the wrong end of a misunderstanding. What did it feel like to be 'in the wrong' and how did it get sorted out?

B. Ask the group to consider this scenario in small groups: a person steals your purse/wallet and you spend all day cancelling your cards and reporting the loss to the police. Later the same day the police phone you and say the thief is in custody. You go down the station to get your property back and learn that the thief wants to apologise to you. How do you feel about that and what would you want to say to the thief or hear from the thief? Is there anything you would want to say to the police?

C. Invite the group to consider this scenario in pairs: your sister has fallen out with the rest of your family. She cuts off communication with you and stops sending cards or presents to you and your children, who don't understand. When your brother gets married she sends a rude letter saying she has no intention of coming to the wedding. Three years later, she suddenly rings up and asks if anyone in the family is still cross with her. What might you say?

2 Going Deeper – Bible Study

You might want to read this passage aloud or organise it as a role play
John 8.1–11 – Woman taken in adultery

But Jesus went to the Mount of Olives. At dawn he appeared again in the temple courts, where all the people gathered around him, and he sat down to teach them. The teachers of the law and the Pharisees brought in a woman caught in adultery. They made her stand before the group and said to Jesus, 'Teacher, this woman was caught in the act of adultery. In the Law Moses commanded us to stone such women. Now what do you say?' They were using this question as a trap, in order to have a basis for accusing him.

But Jesus bent down and started to write on the ground with his finger. When they kept on questioning him, he straightened up and said to them, 'If any one of you is without sin, let him be the first to throw a stone at her.' Again he stooped down and wrote on the ground.

At this, those who heard began to go away one at a time, the older ones first, until only Jesus was left, with the woman still standing there. Jesus straightened up and asked her, 'Woman, where are they? Has no one condemned you?'

'No one, sir,' she said.

'Then neither do I condemn you,' Jesus declared. 'Go now and leave your life of sin.'

○ Who are the Unreconciled in this story and what is their situation?
○ What does this passage teach about condemnation and forgiveness? How does it relate to the world around you today?
○ Why does Jesus say what he does to the woman?
○ What can you learn from this story about how God calls people to do reconciling work among others?

○ Imagine you were the woman, what did you learn from this experience? (For example: The woman meets up with some of her female friends who have seen the incident from afar. What questions might they ask and how might she respond? OR As a group, select various characters in this story, and then mime the whole incident. Afterwards share the emotions and thoughts you experienced in doing this.)

3 Moving On – Task in the Community

Organise an amnesty day or service for your church or fellowship with a version of the 'sorry box' from 'Humanity and God'. Make a space before the altar and invite people to take a symbolic object such as a stone or a ribbon and to think about that object representing whatever they want to be forgiven. The stones, ribbons etc are then placed before the altar as each person says a silent prayer asking for forgiveness. When this is done, the stones, ribbons etc can be made into a pattern or structure. At the conclusion of the service, each person can be given a card or object on the way out which symbolises the assurance of God's forgiveness to all who truly repent.

4 Resting on the way – Theological reflection

Read this story from the Forgiveness Project to the group

A hit and run victim's story

In my work with RoadPeace most of the victims or bereaved families I see say they would like to forgive but can't. However they do eventually reach a place of ease and move beyond anger. Sometimes people tell me that the person who caused the accident hasn't been punished enough. I understand where they're coming from but I always say 'what's enough? No one will ever be punished enough.' Occasionally people really don't want to forgive and I find that sad because I'm in no doubt that not forgiving is detrimental. Bitterness builds up

and spreads out to other people: marriages break up, people fall ill or lose their jobs. I think everyone has the capacity to forgive but they sometimes need help finding those inner resources.

Revd Simon Wilson of RoadPeace, himself a victim of a hit and run accident[1]

. . . .

Ask the group to discuss whether a person can ever be punished 'enough'.

With these things in mind, consider these questions

Where is the seed of new life? What gifts has God given us to offer and receive forgiveness in our own situation?

How will we carry it? What resources will we need to reach out to enable and equip people to journey towards forgiveness in their own lives?

Where can it be born? Identify **one** reconciling action we can commit to which will help Unreconciled people make sense of forgiveness.

How can we nurture it? How can we support that reconciling action and make sure it follows through?

What will we hope to see? What will be changed at the end of this process and what difference should it have made?

5 Gathering Up – Prayer

Lord, When we stand together,
Murmuring at another
Holding our stones,
Feeling them cool and hard in our hands,
Cool the righteous anger in our hearts,
Take the stones from our hand
The planks from our eyes
And let us see you,
Offering your forgiveness
So that we, too, forgive.
Amen

---

1 Story with permission of The Forgiveness Project: www.theforgivenessproject.com.

Session 11: Hell and Heaven

By the end of this session the group will have had opportunity to:

✛ Investigate ideas about hell and heaven and become aware of those living in a hell on earth

✛ Think about hell and heaven in relation to Jesus' parable of the rich man and Lazarus (bible study)

✛ Carry out a simple reconciling task ('a glimpse of heaven') in the community

✛ Reflect theologically on key questions on the hell of the Unreconciled and the reconciled state of heaven

✛ Feed thoughts and ideas into prayer and reflection

The Ladder of Divine Ascent Monastery of St Catherine, Sinai 12th century.

1 Starting Out – Activities

Choose from the selection below

A. Organise a talk from a local history society or get older members of the congregation to talk about what life was like in your area during the Second World War. If your area was bombed, what has happened since to rebuild and reconstruct buildings?

B. Visit a war memorial and make a note of all or some of the names. In pairs write some thoughts or a short letter to the future from the dead person about their hopes and dreams for the survivors of the war.

The Vietnam Veteran's Memorial, Washington, D.C. David Bjorgen.

C. Cut out pictures and headlines from magazines and newspapers or download images from the internet to make a collage to illustrate 'hell on earth'.

○ What would it take to change these images to places of peace and beauty?

○ What organisations and charities are you aware of working for change in this way?

○ Consider how you could offer support or set up a project to make a difference in your local situation.

2 Going Deeper – Bible Study

You might want to read this passage aloud or organise it as a role play

Luke 16:19–31 – The rich man and Lazarus

There was a rich man who was dressed in purple and fine linen and lived in luxury every day. At his gate was laid a beggar named Lazarus, covered with sores and longing to eat what fell from the rich man's table. Even the dogs came and licked his sores.

The time came when the beggar died and the angels carried him to Abraham's side. The rich man also died and was buried. In hell, where he was in torment, he looked up and saw Abraham far away, with Lazarus by his side. So he called to him, 'Father Abraham, have pity on me and send Lazarus to dip the tip of his finger in water and cool my tongue, because I am in agony in this fire.'

Gustave Dore ~ Lazarus and the Rich Man

But Abraham replied, 'Son, remember that in your lifetime you received your good things, while Lazarus received bad things, but now he is comforted here and you are in agony. And besides all this, between us and you a great chasm has been fixed, so that those who want to go from here to you cannot, nor can anyone cross over from there to us.'

He answered, 'Then I beg you, father, send Lazarus to my father's house, for I have five brothers. Let him warn them, so that they will not also come to this place of torment.'

Abraham replied, 'They have Moses and the Prophets; let them listen to them.'

'No, father Abraham,' he said, 'but if someone from the dead goes to them, they will repent.'

He said to him, 'If they do not listen to Moses and the Prophets, they will not be convinced even if someone rises from the dead.'

- ○ Who are the Unreconciled in this story and what is their situation?
- ○ How do you feel about 'they will not be convinced even if someone rises from the dead'? How does that statement relate to the world around us today?
- ○ What is Jesus telling us in this parable about ideas of heaven and hell?
- ○ What can you learn from this parable about how God wants us to behave towards others?
- ○ What do you think might have happened to the five brothers? (For example: the five brothers meet after the burial of their brother and wonder how they should use his wealth which they inherit. Talk through as a small group [each person could be one of the brothers] what they might say to each other, especially as Lazarus and the rich man died around the same time!)

3 Moving On – Task in the Community

Visit a park, heritage site or conservation area. Find an area around the church or in the community – the churchyard, an allotment, or an old shed

and make a project to offer people a 'glimpse of heaven'. This task could also be annexed to a patronal festival, flower or harvest festival, a concert or school event.

4 Resting on the Way – Theological reflection

In the very depths of hell, Dante finds Judas being eternally tortured. Imagine a reunion between Jesus and Judas. What would they say to each other about the events leading to Calvary? Can Judas be saved?

With these things in mind, consider these questions
Where is the seed of new life? What gifts has God given us to become heaven-makers in our own situation?
How will we carry it? What resources will we need to make a difference in our situation and make the world around us more heavenly?
Where can it be born? Identify **one** reconciling action we can commit to which will help to remove the Unreconciled ones from their hell on earth.

How can we nurture it? How can we support that reconciling action and make sure it follows through?

What will we hope to see? What will be changed at the end of this process and what difference should it have made?

5 Gathering Up – Prayer

Lord,
You have not only died,
You have travelled the wastelands of despair,
You opened the gates of hell
And led the hopeless into hope,
Into the brightness of new life.
Help us to follow you even into hell
So that of those given you
We would lose none.
Amen

Books and Resources

Arnold, J. C., (1998) *The Lost Art of Forgiving* (Farmington, PA: The Plough Publishing House)

Aslan, R., (2009) *How to Win a Cosmic War: God, Globalization and the End of the War on Terror* (London: Random House)

Balia D., and Kim, K., *Edinburgh 2010: Witnessing to Christ Today*, Vol. 2 (Oxford: Regnum Books)

Barnes, J., (1989) *A History of the World in 10 ½ Chapters* (London: Jonathan Cape)

Boff, L., (1988) *Trinity and Society* (Maryknoll: Orbis)

Bosch, D., (1991) *Transforming Mission: Paradigm Shifts in Theology of Mission* (Maryknoll, NY: Orbis Books)

Brueggemann, W., (1978) *The Prophetic Imagination* (Minneapolis: Fortress Press)

Buchan, T., (2004) *"Blessed is he who has brought Adam from Sheol": Christ's descent to the dead in the theology of St Ephrem the Syrian* (Piscataway, NJ: Gorgia's Press)

Cameron, D., (1985) *Feminism and Linguistic Theory* (Basingstoke: Macmillan)

Cassidy, S., (1994) *Light from the Dark Valley: Reflections on Suffering and the Care of the Dying* (Notre dame, Indiana: Ave Maria Press)

Castle, B., (2008) *Reconciling One and All: God's Gift to the World* (London: SPCK)

Church of England Board of Social Responsibility, (1999) *Prisons, a study in vulnerability* (London: Church House Publishing)

Citizens Online and National Centre for Social Research (2008) *Digital Exclusion Profiling of Vulnerable Groups: ex-offenders* (London: HMSO)

Daly, G., (1998) 'Forgiveness and Community' in Alan Falconer (ed) *Reconciling Memories* (Dublin: Columba Press)

Doctrine Commission of the Church of England (1995) *The Mystery of Salvation* (London: Church House Publishing)

Elsner, A., (2008) *The Gates of Injustice* (New Jersey: Pearson Education Limited)

Enright, R., and North, J., (Eds) (1998) *Exploring Forgiveness* (Madison, WI: University of Wisconsin Press)

Evans, A., (2004) *Healing Liturgies for the Seasons of Life* (Louisville: Westminster John Knox Press)

Federal Writers Project, South Carolina, (1937) *Twenty-One Negro Spirituals* (New York: Viking Press): online at http://newdeal.feri.org/texts/612.htm

Ford, D., (1997) *The Shape of Living* (London: Fount paperbacks)

Ford, D., (1999) *Self and Salvation, being transformed* (Cambridge: Cambridge University Press)

Forrester, D., (1997) *Christian Justice and Public Policy* (Cambridge: Cambridge University Press)

Fortune, M., (1991) 'Forgiveness, the last step', in *Violence in the Family: A workshop curriculum for clergy and other helpers* (Cleveland, Ohio: The Pilgrim Press)

Fung, R., (1992) *The Isaiah Vision: an ecumenical strategy for congregational evangelism*, (Geneva: WCC Publications)

Gaarder, J., (1998) *Through a Glass Darkly* (London: Orion)

Girard, R., (1978) *Things Hidden Since the Foundation of the World* (trans. Stephen Bann and Michael Meteer) (London: Athlone Books)

Griffith, L., (1993) *The Fall of the Prison: Biblical Perspectives on Prison Abolition* (Grand Rapids: Wm B.Eerdmans)

Hunter, L., (1953) *The Seed and the Fruit* (London: SCM)

Jenkins, T., (1999) *Religion in Everyday English Life: an Ethnographic Approach* (Oxford: Berghahn Books)

Johnson, V., 'Towards a Liturgical Missiology: A Trinitarian Framework for Worship, Mission and Pastoral Care', *Anaphora*, 2:2 (2008)

Jones, G., (1995) *Embodying Forgiveness, a Theological Analysis* (Grand Rapids, Michigan: Eerdmans)

Juergensmeyer, M., (2000) *Terror in the Mind of God: The Global Rise of Religious Violence* (Berkeley: University of California Press)

Kay, R., (2000) *Saul* (New York: St Martin's Press)

Kim, K., (ed) (2005) *Reconciling Mission The Ministry of Healing and Reconciliation in the Church Worldwide* (Delhi: ISPCK)

Kim, S., Kollontai, P., and Hoyland, G., (eds) (2008) *Peace and Reconciliation: In Search of Shared Identity* (Farnham: Ashgate)

Kureishi, H., (new edition 1999) *Intimacy* (London: Faber)

Lawrence, L., (2009) *The Word in Place: Reading the New Testament in Contemporary Contexts* (London: SPCK)

Linn, M., Fabricant, S., Linn, D., (1997) *Don't Forgive Too Soon* (Mahwah, NJ: Paulist Press)

Luskin, F., (2002) *Forgive For Good* (San Francisco: Harper)

Mandela, N., (1995) *A Long Walk to Freedom* (New York: Back Bay Books)

Marshall, C., (2001) *Beyond Retribution: A New Testament Vision for Justice, Crime and Punishment* (GrandRapids: Wm. B. Eerdmans)

Marshall, C., (2002) 'Prison, Prisoners and the Bible' a paper delivered to 'Breaking Down the Walls' Conference, Tukua Nga Here Kia Marama Ai Matamata, 14–16 June, 2002 online at http://www.restorativejustice.org/10fulltext/marshall-christopher.-prison-prisoners-and-the-bible

Matar, D., (2010) *What it means to be Palestinian, Stories of Palestinian Peoplehood* (London: I.B.Tauris)

Matthey, J., (2004) 'Reconciliation, *Missio Dei* and the Church's Mission' in Mellor, H., and Yates, T. (eds.), *Mission, Violence and Reconciliation* (Sheffield: Cliff College Publishing)

Milbank, J., (2003) *Being Reconciled: Ontology and Pardon* (London: Routledge)

Moltmann, J., (1974) *The Crucified God* (London: SCM)

Müller-Fahrenholtz, G., (1997) *The Art of Forgiveness* (Geneva: WCC Publications)

Pratt, J., (2008) 'Retribution and Retaliation' in S Giora Shoham, Ori Beck and Martin Kett (eds) *International Handbook of Penology and Criminal Justice* (Boca Raton, Florida: CRC Press)

Reducing Re-offending by ex-prisoners, summary of Social Exclusion Unit report 2002 online at http://www.thelearningjourney.co.uk/reducing_report.pdf/file_view

Responding to Domestic Abuse: guidelines for those with pastoral responsibilities, London: Church House Publishing 2006, available online at http://www.churchofengland.org/our-views/marriage,-family-and-sexuality-issues/domestic-abuse.aspx

Rider Upton, J., (1999) *Time for Embracing: Reclaiming Reconciliation* (Collegeville, MN: Liturgical Press)

Rosenberg, M., (2nd edition 2003) *Nonviolent Communication: a Language of Life* (Encinitas: Puddledancer Press).

Sacks, O., (1985) *The Man Who Mistook His Wife for a Hat* (London: Picador 1986 edition)

Said, E., (1990) 'Reflections on Exile' in Russell Ferguson, William Olander, Trinh T. Minh-Ha and Cornel West, *Out There: Marginalisation and Contemporary Cultures* (Cambridge, Mass: MIT Press)

Schreiter, R., (1992) *Reconciliation: Mission and Ministry in a Changing Social Order* (Maryknoll, NY: Orbis)

Schreiter, R., (1998) *The Ministry of Reconciliation: Spirituality and Strategies* (Maryknoll, NY: Orbis)

Schreiter, R., (2004) 'The Theology of Reconciliation and Peacemaking for Mission' in Mellor, H., and Yates, T. (eds.) *Mission, Violence and Reconciliation* (Sheffield: Cliff College Publishing)

Schreiter, R., (2005) 'Reconciliation and Healing as a Paradigm for Mission' in *International Review of Mission*, January 2005 Volume 94, Issue 372, pp. 74–83

Sedgwick, P., (ed 2004) *Re-thinking Sentencing* (London: Church House Publishing)

Selvanayagam, I., 'Gal-ed versus Peniel: True reconciliation in the Esau-Jacob/Israel story' in Kirsteen Kim (ed), (2005) *Reconciling Mission: The Ministry of Healing and Reconciliation in the Church Worldwide* (Delhi: ISPCK)

Snyder, R., (2001) *The Protestant Ethic and the Spirit of Punishment* (Grand Rapids, Michigan:

Eerdmans)

Song, C. S., (1979) *Third Eye Theology: Theology in Formation in Asian Settings* (Maryknoll, NY: Orbis Books)

Song, C. S., (1986) *Theology from the Womb of Asia* (Maryknoll, NY: Orbis Books)

Stott, J., (1986) *The Cross of Christ* (Nottingham: Inter-Varsity Press)

Taylor, J., (1998) *The Uncancelled Mandate* (London: Church House Publishing)

Tutu, D., (1999) *No Future Without Forgiveness* (London: Rider, Random House)

Tweed, T., (2006) *Crossing and Dwelling, a theory of religion* (Cambridge, Mass.: Harvard University Press)

Vizenor, G., (ed) (1998) *Survivance, Narratives of Native Presence* (Lincoln, NE: University of Nebraska Press)

Volkan, V., (2006) *Killing in the Name of Identity: A Study of Bloody Conflicts* (Charlottesville, VA: Pitchstone Publishing)

Volf, M., (1996) *Exclusion & Embrace – A Theological Exploration of Identity, Otherness and Reconciliation.* (Nashville, TN: Abingdon Press)

WCC (2009) 'Re-visioning justice from the margins of the new world of 21st century', online at: http://www.oikoumene.org/en/resources/documents/wcc-programmes/unity-mission-evangelism-and-spirituality/just-and-inclusive-communities/rio-report-re-visioning-justice-from-the-margins.html

Webster, A., (2009) *You are Mine Reflections on Who We Are* (London: SPCK)

Wink, W., (1992) *Engaging the Powers*, (Minneapolis: Fortress Press)

Wolterstorff, N., (1987) *Lament for a Son* (Grand Rapids: Eerdmans)

Young, J., 'Charles Young and the American Prison Experiment: the dilemmas of a libertarian' online at http://www.malcolmread.co.uk/JockYoung/murray.htm

Some useful websites

www.cnvc.org

www.contemporarychristianity.org.

www.cvsni.org

www.presenceandengagement.org.uk

http://www.prisonfellowship.org.uk/sycamore-tree.html

http://www.arocha.org

www.stethelburgas.org

www.peacebuilding.caritas.org

www.wiscomp.org/peaceprints.htm

www.trc10.co.za/index.html

www.theforgivenessproject.com

www.victimsupport.org.uk

www.amnesty.org.uk

Acknowledgements

Every effort has been made to verify the accuracy of previously published text, quotations and other material used in this book, and to obtain permissions where appropriate. The publishers will be pleased to rectify any errors or omissions in future editions of this book.

Images have been drawn from many of the free resouces of sites such as Flickr, Morguefile, etc., as well as from Shutterstock and Corbis; the credits have been attributed as directed and the following refers to the images by page number (errors or omissions will be corrected in future editions of this book):

p.vi–Morguefile_NasirKhan; p.xvi–Cincinnati blight and renewal: Derek Jensen; p.4–U.S. Army Sergeant Kornelia Rachwal gives a young Pakistani girl a drink of water: Technical Sergeant Mike Buytas; p.11–Spiral galaxy courtesy Nasa and Michelangelo Wiki Commons; p.21–Manheim, Michael Philip, 1940– , Two Long-Time Residents of Neptune Road_412-DA-5995_US National Archives_Flickr; p.23–A Mothers Love IV_ron.stinson, morguefile; p.31–shutterstock_22606435~Distinctive Images; p.35–Truth and lies, by Chelle, Morguefile; p.36–Christian Witness from A Glass Darkly blog by Dennis Haack; p.43–The Yorck Project: Vincent van Gogh, 1890. Kröller-Müller Museum. The Good Samaritan (after Delacroix); p.44–Children's section of Camargo graveyard, by Tomas Castelazo; p.53–shutterstock_35040019©Zygalski Krzysztof; p.55–Statue of Nelson Mandela by Ian Walters in London by Fearless Fred; p.69–Riot Police in Edinburgh G8 Demonstration, Dave Morris; p.84–Morguefiel; p.89–A candle for prisoners of conscience in Salisbury Cathedral, by Simon Beer for Amnesty International. Courtesy wikimedia commons, Gunnar Bach Pedersen; p.94–Skulls at a memorial site in rural Rwanda: Corbis; p.103–Refugees cross from DR Congo into Uganda at the border village of Busanza by Sam DCruz, Shutterstock; p.108–forgive by onkel wart, morguefile; p.112–forgive by JOPHIELsmiles, Flickr; p.113–Ravensbruck ©Marius Mézerette/Fotopedia; p.126–Hands reaching out from Hell at Wat Rong Khun in Chiang Rai, shutterstock ©bumihills; p.136–Eden Project, ©Kevin Britland/shutterstock; p.147–Glasgow tenements on black, 2006. ©Kenny Muir; p.158–Pontius Pilate's "What is Truth?" – stylized inscription at entrance to Antoni Gaudi's Sagrada Família, by Etan J. Tal (Barcelona); p.160–Child soldiers in the Central African Republic, Pierre Holtz / UNICEF CAR; p.170–Rescue workers – Asianet-Pakistan/shutterstock; p.180–Portrait of burn survivor, Corbis; p.198–The Vietnam Veteran's Memorial, Washington, D.C., David Bjorgen, morguefile;